William H. Brown

Plain Facts for Farmers, Horticulturists and Gardeners

William H. Brown

Plain Facts for Farmers, Horticulturists and Gardeners

ISBN/EAN: 9783337083359

Printed in Europe, USA, Canada, Australia, Japan

Cover: Foto ©Lupo / pixelio.de

More available books at **www.hansebooks.com**

PLAIN FACTS

For Farmers, Horticulturists and Gardeners

PROF. W. H. BROWN'S

INSECTICIDE RECIPES
(IN SOLID FORM)

A SURE PRESERVATOR OF

Orchards, Gardens, Parks and Pleasure Grounds

AND HOW TO CARE FOR THEM.

INCLUDING THIRTY-FIVE OF THE BEST KNOWN RECIPES FOR THE DESTRUCTION OF INSECT PESTS.

A Brief History of the Insects That Destroy Vegetation.

Testimonials to the Medicine That Kills Them.

BY

W. H. BROWN

1894
ACME PUBLISHING COMPANY
SEATTLE

W. H. BROWN

INTRODUCTORY.

The history of horticulture from the first has been fraught with difficulties. To care for and dress the garden was one of the commands given to our first parents, and the experience of all engaged in this, one of the noblest occupations entrusted to man, has been one of unceasing care and toil. Like the disease of sin in the human soul, the destructive diseases and pests of the horticulturists are omnipresent, and are seeking to destroy the noblest and best to be found, and as the battle has ever been on in the contest in the human soul between the evil and the good, so has the battle ever been on between the horticulturist and the pestiferous insects and deadly diseases that are seeking to destroy the product of his labor.

In late years, so great has become the fruit growing industry, of our country, and so multiplied have become the enemies that are battling its onward march, that sumptuary laws have been enacted by many states and counties, and boards of commissioners have been created for the special purpose of enforcing them, and large sums of money have been expended in experimenting for the purpose of discovering the best remedies to be used in combatting the destructive pests of orchard and field and farm.

Men have made it their life work studying out the most effective means of preventing and destroying the pests that are devastating the years of honest earnest labor on our orchards and farms. The author of this book has devoted the best years of his life to these investigations. He has studied the habits and life of the pests and familiarized himself with their method of attack on tree life; he has also examined into the requirements of vegetation to resist these attacks.

These investigations have resulted in one of the most important discoveries of the times—a compound known as W. H. Brown's Insect Exterminator—which has been patented and is being successfully and generally introduced all over the country. His work has not been circumscribed by limited experimental ground, but it has been in the broader field of the nursery and the orchard, in nearly every State in the Union. He has combatted the insects on their native heath, at their strongest points, from the frigid north to the citrus belts of the semi-tropics, and in every section and on every insect his preparation has proved effective in the greatest degree. While this solution has been formulated to destroy any insect that infests trees or fruits, it does it without the least injury to tree or fruit.

The author takes great pleasure in calling the attention of the reader to the numerous testimonials in this publication. They are only samples of many more of the same class that he is receiving daily.

A. N. HAMILTON.

SKETCH OF THE AUTHOR'S LIFE.

After the introduction so kindly given by my friend Col. Hamilton, I can simply inform my readers that I was born of Scotch-Irish parents, in the township of Chatham, Lower Canada, on the 12th of March, 1842. Being born eight days after the inauguration of Gen. W. H. Harrison, I was named after this statesman, of whom I have always been proud, and doubly so since I had the honor of casting a vote for his illustrious grandson, Gen. Harrison, Jr.

At the age of four years my parents moved to Western Canada, and at six years old I was left fatherless, my father receiving his death from a falling log, while helping a neighbor erect a log house. My mother being left with five small children was forced to find homes for them, and owing to the fact that most of my relatives lived in the far distant East, the mode of travel made it impossible to reach them. Three children were placed with relatives, and two with strangers, my lot being cast with the latter. My adopted uncle being an educated horticulturist, having but one child, a woman grown, I was soon placed in a nursery row with pruning knife in hand. So great was my love for this profession that I soon had many fence corners planted with rejected trees. Here I stayed for six years. There being no children to play with, I can simply recall my childhood days with playmates such as trees, shrubs, plants and flowers, and insects of every kind and description that I could find, and in fact frogs, toads and other reptiles did not escape my notice. All seemed to me to be natural beauties, and I can now recall those days as being the happiest ones of my life. During these six years of my life I had not attended school a day; I had not even been taught the alphabet. My mother being college educated and who had seen better days, taught school four years, after which she married quite a wealthy English horticulturist. I studied my profession under this gentleman for at least three years, attending school winters, after which I worked for my board most of the time. When in my twentieth year I commenced the study of theology. In the campaign for Lincoln and Douglas for President, I took an active part, and being in Illinois I carried the wide awake flag for Old Abe. I did some stumping for the successful President. I stated to an audience of at least 5,000 citizens at Jenera, Ill., that I had carried both flag and torch for Old Abe, and if elected by the voice of the American people and it became necessary, I would carry the bayonet to sustain him. I made my word good by enlisting in Company G, 52nd Illinois Infantry, on the 22nd day of September. 1861. Refusing a captain's commission in the 58th Illinois, I accepted the rank of a private, so as to get with boys with whom I had an acquaintance. I was standing picket with not a dry stitch on me when I was taken sick with the measles, with which I came very near dying. I returned to my regiment just in time for the battle of Shiloh, where I was wounded on the afternoon of the first day's fight and was sent to Evansville, Ind.; taken out of the hospital by Mrs. Doctor Castleberry and Mayor Baker's daughter, who was Mrs. Castleberry's niece. Being placed in a palace sick-room there I lay for two and a half months, at times given up to die by my physician, Dr. Milhasen, who kindly tendered his services gratuitously. These two ladies and Grandmother Castleberry, assisted by the young ladies of the female college, were the angels of mercy who administered to my wants in a strange land. The doctor said that the reason that I didn't die, was that I would have kicked twice after I was dead. But had it not been for those ladies I would have made the two last kicks. Therefore the readers of this sketch can always count on me in favor of woman suffrage. I returned to my regiment and was on the march to Iuka. My regiment took no part in the fight. I was in the second battle of Corinth and was on special service for eighteen months.

I visited Old Abe in the White House, and was dismissed from the service by surgeon's Certificate of Disability, June, '64. I have been pensioned by the Republican administration at $8 per month, raised to $14 per month under Cleveland, and I still live. I can assure the readers of this short narrative of my war experience, I can only express my true feelings with a tear when I pen the language of the poet:

> "Under the roses the blue,
> Under the lilies the gray,
> Under the sod and the dew,
> Waiting the judgment day."

I married my first wife, Miss Alvira Walker, soon after my discharge. She died three months after marriage, of typhoid fever. Returned home to Canada and attended school one and a half years. My health failed and I gave up a college course. After four years I married my present wife, whose maiden name was Miss Amelia W. Clark, and who I have always found to be true to her marriage vows, cheerful in prosperity, and always speaking comfort in time of adversity. To us one child has been born, Helen E. Brown, who is and always has been the cheer of the house. She is past 18 years old, has played the organ in church since she was 12 years old and is ever found at her post as a Christian worker. I can say for her what few fathers can say of an only child, she has the first impudent word to give me at this writing.

I have given the greater part of my past life to the study of nature, this being my chief enjoyment, and I have a longing desire to live long enough to see my efforts in the destruction of noxious insects become a boon to humanity.

ENTOMOLOGY—INSECT LIFE.

I cannot conceive of any subject more prolific of astonishing revealments to an inquiring mind than the study of entomology. Environed as we are by finitism, we cannot conceive of alpha or omega. To us as creatures creative of terra period there seems to be no beginning of life or ending of re-creation. Yesterday an inert body, to-day it becomes a loathsome worm, bringing ruin and devastation to the vegetable kingdom and laying waste the prospective millions of man. To-morrow this wonderful destroyer becomes a beautiful butterfly, with velvety wings more beautiful than can be painted by the hand of man or described by the pen of the scribe. As they are carried by their beautiful wings, like the humming-bird sipping the honey from the beautiful flowers that ornament nature's Eden, and so we exclaim, ad infinitum. Yet for all this fitful kaleidoscopic change we can and do, in the study of this lower life, grasp with a knowledge through entomological research, an escape from a surcease of what otherwise would have been a mystery for all time. After a careful study of this subject for more than 40 years, I have as yet failed, in my opinion, to have learned more than a part of the alphabet, when I take into consideration the fact that in order to be life there must be a living germ, so says reason and so says scientific research. Nevertheless, let me ask why is it? Suppose a man in the prime of life to be cut down by a bullet or buried alive in a metallic casket six feet under ground, when decomposition takes place his flesh becomes a crawling mass of worms, making and confirming the truthfulness of Holy Writ where it says that " dust we are and unto dust we shall return", and that "we are worms of the soil and we shall be devoured by worms." Taking into consideration the wonderful works of nature, I am led to exclaim in the language of the poet :

"God moves in a mysterious way his wonders to perform,
He plants his footstep in the sea and rides upon the storm.

> Deep in unfathomable minds, of never fading skill,
> He treasures up His bright desires and works His sovereign will."

It is enough for man to know that the great majority of insect life is man's great enemy, and that to see an army of insects is to see an army of foes, and how to declare a successful warfare against this enemy in the United States is a question yet to be solved. I make this stasement from the fact that in the last four years the State Boards alone have paid out for the extermination of the insect foe in the United States hundreds of thousands of dollars, and still their onward march seems to be to victory.

It is not the aim of the writer to enter into a scientific history of insect life, as there are any number of such works. My aim is to give to my readers something of a practical nature; something to show that when they see a butterfly they almost invariably see a foe, as they are the parents of the many worms that do the work as destroyers. That when they see a bug, look out for the enemy, as they are the insect that produce the grub that destroy the tree, shrub and vegetation in many instances. That when they see the fly they see the parent of the magot, and so I might go on until I wrote a book. Perhaps some of my readers might say, you mention the worm, you mention the grub and the maggot. I want to know the difference, as they all look alike to me. Well, I will not go to Webster's unabridged to learn some words that I never learned in school, so as to twist the tongue of the farmer who might undertake to read the names, I will simply refer to a few true insects that are most destructive to man's welfare. A butterfly, while a worm, is called a caterpillar. This caterpillar while in this stage of life has six real legs, and usually four false ones, which are simply dots of flesh. By being careful in examination of an insect, it is an easy matter to come to a correct decision as to what kind of an insect you may have to contend with. A beetle while in the worm state hasn't the sign of a leg, so it is quite easy to distinguish the difference. The worm in its larvae state is called a grub; it is much thicker and usually shorter than a worm. Maggots are the skippers or flyblows; they don't need further explanation.

PLANTING AN ORCHARD.

Where to plant and how to plant, and what kind of trees to plant, are questions often asked of me by men who are going into this business. Where to plant, is a question that carries more weight with it than many other subjects, from the fact that different climates often speak louder than words. For instance, you may plant an orchard on a hill-side, sloping to the southwest, any place in the Puget Sound country, and you meet with success, so far as location is concerned—for this reason, a fruit tree requires considerable sunlight and moderately dry weather, which is not always attainable on the Sound, more especially on a north slope. Then another trouble you will have to contend with, your trees will soon be covered with a green moss (fungus) which is very injurious to them. While east of the mountains in Oregon, Washington and Idaho, this theory will not hold good, from the fact that they have too much dry weather in some instances. Another reason why an orchard should not be planted on a south or southwestern slope, in a dry and colder climate is that the orchardist has to contend with cold, changeable winters. I don't claim that it is the cold that injures the trees; I claim that it is the thawing and freezing combined that does the damage. For instance, it has been cold, freezing weather, the mercury standing at 10 degrees below zero (perhaps not so cold) for some little time. A sudden change takes place—the weather gets warm, the frost is hurried out of the trees by the sun, up goes the sap from the roots and the buds begin to swell. All nature looks as if spring had returned with all its beauties. All at once another change takes place—in one night the thermometer registers zero, or perhaps below. The sap that began to flow came to an instantaneous standstill, more especially on the south side of the tree. The sap remains in the stock, limbs and buds of the tree in a dormant condition for days. Finally there is a gradual thaw. The frozen sap that has no business there thaws out; it has no way of escape, finally it becomes impure, sours in the sap-lining, nature's blood vessels are clogged with impure blood (sap) forcing its way upward, still upward, mixing the pure sap with the impure, it finally reaches the buds (lungs); nature having but little vitality left fails to throw off the impurities. The consequence is, the tree sooner or later dies in the contest for life, while trees planted on a northern or northwestern slope have not been effected by these sudden changes, from the fact that the heat on this particular occasion having never reached them. The reader well knows that the snow is all gone on the south slope when it has hardly commenced melting on the north slope.

Another question may be asked by the reader: "Suppose I have my orchard planted on a south slope, what is to be done in this case? Can my trees be saved?" My answer is, they can to a very great extent, if attended to in time—that is before the tree or trees have received their death warrant. The first thing to be done in this case is to trim the new growth back before the tree stops growing in the fall so as to harden what is left of the new growth. The less water the roots get late in the fall the better. Just before winter or freezing weather sets in, mulch well around the roots with coarse barn-yard manure, but be careful not to let the manure come in contact with the stock of the tree. Take two pieces of board about 10 inches wide; nail them together, giving them the appearance of a house roof at one third pitch; sharpen at one end; drive the sharpened end into the ground about eight inches from the base of the tree, letting the top rest against the trunk of the tree at or in the branches. This protects the tree from the sun and will prevent thawing. This prescription will do more to save your orchard than anything you can do under the circumstances.

I am often asked, Which is the best place to plant an orchard, on the hill-side or in the valley? When climate is not brought into question, my answer to this question is, so far as the Puget Sound country is concerned and other similar countries, owing to the fact of their great annual rainfall and the fertility of their valleys, trees planted in those valleys make a too rapid growth, are too susceptible to wind and weather and in consequence the trees are shortlived, owing to the fact that they overbear; therefore they come into existence quick and in consequence go out in the same way.

Such countries as Eastern Oregon, Washington, Idaho, Utah and other sections where they depend on irrigation and where their winters are severe, I would advise the planting of apple orchards as much as possible on the side hills, commencing lower down on the side-hill and extending further down into the valley, planting prunes, peaches and such kind of fruit in the lowest land. One important feature must not be lost sight of, no matter where the orchard is planted, and that is natural drainage. California is, in many instances, an exception to the general rule. Take the Eastern States, such as Indiana, Michigan, Ohio, Western Canada and all the Southern States. Where their fruit is failing it is not so much climatic changes that ails them as it is insects.

How to plant, is the next question that presents itself.

First prepare your ground so that when it is ready it will look as if a newly sowed crop had been planted. Mark off your ground, as for corn, 33 feet between hills for apple, cherry and pear. For prune, plum, peach and other fruits of a similar nature, from 25 to 30 feet will do as well. After the ground has been prepared and the marking done, then hole-digging is next in order. The larger a hole is dug the better, using judgment. But don't dig less than 12 inches deep and 24 in diameter, digging the sides perpendicular. If there is any noticeable slope let the slope be so as to make the bottom larger than the top. This being done, the next thing in order is tree getting. But a very important part is what varieties or what kind to get, and it is a question that no man can answer, not knowing where the trees are to be planted. Trees that will do well in the East, in many instances, will not do well in the West. Trees that are a success in the South are a failure in the North. So it is. Therefore for me to attempt to answer that question, would be absurd on my part. There is one sure rule to go by, that is: What apples or fruit sell so as to bring the most money in the Eastern market is what you want. Be sure they are good keepers and shippers, and that these kinds do well in your locality. Spend some little time investigating this question. The next thing to be done after a decision has been reached, is to decide how many kinds to get and how many of each kind to get.

This question can be easily answered, that is if you are intending to become a fruit shipper. Select a few of the best kinds, get enough of any one kind so that if an order comes for a car load, you will have them to ship without running all over among your neighbors, picking a few bushels here and a few bushels there to fill out your order, as these dealers are all business, and they want their orders filled, and that at once.

Now comes the getting of the trees. Where to get them is a very important question. My advice is to see the stock, if it is convenient, and if you have a home nursery in reach, go personally and make your selection. If not, find out how you can communicate with the best nursery and to them give your order. One great reason that it is better to make your selection in person, is that in tree shipping time the nurseryman is very busy, for the season is short. Sometimes he gets too many irons in the fire, and some, through poor apprentices get burnt (I mean the roots) and the honest nurseryman is called dishonest.

The first thing, if it is an apple tree you want, ask to be shown his two-year-olds, then satisfy yourself that they are two-year-olds as they may be stunted three- or four-year-olds. Look and you will usually tell by the swirl or thimble-like appearance where the new growth commenced the previous year on the stock. Don't get a stunted tree, as you can't make a first class cow out of a stunted calf, neither can you make an old man a young one.

The next thing, see them dug. Don't let the roots be mutilated. Look to it that you get all the young fibre roots you can with them. Don't expose the roots to the air more than is necessary. Have them taken immediately into the packing-shed out of the wind and weather. After this has been done, commence a general inspection of each tree separately; look at the buds on the tender growth; see that no little shiny, black egg is deposited in the crevices around the limbs; if so, these are probably eggs of the aphis or green louse. Perhaps you may see some little red eggs, if so, you have probably found the deposit of the red spider. See that the bark is smooth and clean and free from any foreign substance. Take a first class look at the stock, see that there are no lumps or roughness that don't belong there. Now look the roots over carefully and see if you can find lumps like small or large warts; if so, ask the nurseryman what that means. If he says nothing, then see if you can't show him some little lice around the knots; then ask him what they are. If he says that he don't know, tell him they have the woolly aphis, and that you don't want such stock. If he and you have settled this difficulty by a compromise (which would have been hard to perfect had it been in my case) next look and see if you have a sickly tree in the lot. Cut off a limb and see if the pith is the natural color. See if the wood around the pith is not discolored. Ask what that means. Then split the tree down the centre and see if it is not black all the way down; if so, the tree has the "black-heart." Don't buy black-hearted trees from any man, and I am positive that an honest man would not want you to. Nevertheless those diseases are being scattered broadcast. My main object in giving the purchaser the advice that I have in purchasing his bill of trees, is the fact that a poor lot of trees would be dear if he got them for nothing.

In concluding this subject let me say. Having dwelt at some length in the way of cautioning my readers against infested nursery stock and in so doing I have attributed all the blame to the nurseryman, therefore if I have laid all the blame where it belongs I have imposed no injustice. If I have not, then I am guilty of unjust dealing between man and man. My aim is and always has been to deal fairly, setting forth facts as they are. The nurseryman is required to disinfect his nursery stock, which he does in complying to the letter of the law, and his stock is perfectly clean. He has a large shipment to some large fruit growing community; therefore it becomes necessary to secure a distributing point. He secures it on some vacant lot in some large city, where it is most convenient for all his customers. The trenches are dug, the trees, shrubs and plants healed in. After he has had time to breathe he begins to look at his surroundings. What does he find? He finds that his fine clean nursery stock, of which he was so proud, has been shipped into a pest-house for distribution to his customers. A person might just as well take up his abode in a house of ill repute and expect to come out virtuous, as to have to heal in or plant trees in such a place without injury. But who is to blame for this state of affairs? It is the man who exacted of the producer compliance with the law, and let corporations pass comparatively unnoticed. Let there be fair dealing in this matter.

After the receipt of the trees, place the boxes under cover, open and cut all mutilated roots from the under side with a sharp knife, make a slanting, smooth cut so that when placed in the ground, the wound will rest on the ground. Aftert his has been done, dampen the roots well, place them in a conveyance, throw wet blankets over them, then proceed to plant them. Be very careful to get every variety by itself. Don't make a mistake in this part of the work. Plant them in straight rows each way without fail. I don't suppose the apples would be any more crooked, but it is so much more pleasing to the eye of the passer-by to see nice, straight rows. I believe that California beats the world for straight rows in planting.

The first thing to do in planting is to fill up the hole with loose earth so that when the tree is placed in the hole ready for planting it will be about the depth it stood when in the nursery row. Straighten all roots, placing them as near as possible as you would suppose them to have stood while in the nursery. After this has been done, fill in about three inches of fine loam, then pour in two pails of water (or perhaps less will do). Take hold of stock, churn it up and down just enough to settle the wet earth around the roots, then throw in another half pail of water. Go on with planting, giving the water in the previous hole time to settle, return, fill up around the tree, tramping gently so as to pack the earth evenly around the roots and stock. This process of planting will have caused the tree to settle about two inches deeper than when placed on the loose earth in the hole. In this way plant your orchard and your tree planting will be done right.

In case you have a dry climate, it is sometimes best to put a little coarse mulching around the roots or base of the tree, but be sure and don't let the mulching come in contact with the stock. If you don't have frequent rains during the first four months after planting, water so as to wet the roots every ten or twelve days, after which, with good luck, you may count on your orchard as being a grand success.

The next thing to be considered is how to cultivate.

Here is where orchardists differ very much. Some believe in the old practice of sowing grain in it; others in planting hoed crops; others no crops at all. I believe in the latter, and I find my opinion endorsed by the large majority of the great fruit-growers in California and elsewhere. But if you plant any crop, plant a hoed crop the first three years, after that none at all; then keep your orchard clean and well cultivated; don't let a spear of grass or weed grow and you will be well paid for your trouble.

Don't let any kind of stock run in your orchard. Some advise letting hogs run in an orchard, the object being that hogs will eat all wormy apples. This may be so, but I hold an orchard in too high esteem to make a hog pasture of it. I would advise picking up the wind-falls and feeding to the hogs in a pasture made for that purpose. Hens should have free access to the orchard, from the fact that they pick up many worms and beetles that are much better in a hen's stomach than depositing eggs by the hundreds on your apple trees; therefore the more hens and birds you may have in your orchard the better—that is, if they don't lay claim to the fruit.

A few practicable suggestions as to how and when to prune an orchard:

The best time to prune is just before the sap starts. How to prune is greatly governed by climate, but there is one general rule which should always be observed in every climate, never allow one limb to cross another and grow that way. Always prune so as to reduce your tree to one general perpendicular trunk. Cut back new growths on apples one-third and prunes about one-half. This will cause the limbs to grow not so long but will increase in diameter. Never let your trees grow so that you can't pick the fruit from a step-ladder not over twelve feet in length, for two reasons: One is that it is much easier to pick the fruit than if allowed to grow higher. Another reason, if troubled with insects you can get at them while spraying, with much more ease from the umbrella shaped top. Don't trim so as to have all stock and no top. Form first branches, as a rule, five feet from the ground, somewhat owing to the natural shape of the tree. If your orchard is in a hot, dry climate let the limbs grow so as to form a pretty dense foliage. If in a wet climate, cut out branches so as to let in more sunlight. Don't let suckers grow at the base, as they sap the life out of the tree and make a harbor for insects. Never cut off a limb that is an inch in diameter without putting hot grafting wax on the wound. These suggestions, if followed, will keep your orchard in pretty good shape.

FERTILIZERS.

I have in my travels seen many orchards that have stood perhaps a quarter of a century, they having been noted for their fine fruit, both as regards abundance and quality. Now they are failing and failing fast. The owners of these fine orchards, being aware of the fact, lay the cause to old age, while the facts are, these orchards are only in the prime of life. One fact I wish to be stamped in the minds of our American horticulturists with a stamp of an indelible nature, and that is the importance of the use of fertilizers. I find in my travels those who don't seem to know what ruin the lack of manure brings to the tree, the shrub or the plant. I sincerely hope that the time will soon come when the American orchardist will open his eyes more to the benefit of fertilizers, as they have in some parts of Europe, where they have the Egyptian mummies shipped in by the train load, ground into bone dust, then used as a fertilizer at the roots of everything of a horticultural nature. I imagine I can hear some lady reader exclaim, "Oh, horror, can that be possible?" From what I can learn it is a fact, and to my mind it only establishes two facts—one, that bone-dust must be good; another, that God never fails to make good his promises to man. He said to man, "Dust thou art and to dust thou shalt return." I hope that I have not failed to establish the fact on the minds of every one who reads this, that bone-meal makes a fine fertilizer.

There is another thing that I have noticed in my travels, that the farmer usually builds his barn on a side-hill, the object being to have good drainage. This I don't object to if he has a good cistern at the lower side to catch all the liquid as it goes down hill, for it would do the roots of the trees more good than the stream below, especially if his cattle drink out of the same stream. One instance was brought to my notice while in Nebraska, last summer. In the farming community with which I had long formed acquaintance, those who kept clean barnyards waxed rich, while those who did not became poorer and poorer. One very remarkable instance was where there were two neighborhoods, one strictly American, the other strictly Holland-Dutch. I became acquainted with those people, and when asked by an American to take a meal with him or stay over night, my horse was fed in some kind of a shack, while I partook of my meal in a good residence. On the other hand, the same hospitality was extended to me by my Holland friends, my horse was conducted into a good barn, to partake of a sumptuous meal, while I was conducted into a dug-out to partake of mine. Now, let me ask, what changes have come about in the lapse of a few years? The fact is, the Hollanders who lived in dug-outs now have fine houses and barns, and the young Hollanders have taken possession of their neighbors' farms and are moving on to prosperity, as did their predecessors. Their American friends have moved West to grow up with the country, making good in another instance, the parable of the many and few talents. It is not my aim to show to my readers what the manural properties of bone may be, whether it is nitrogen and phosphoric acid, by which the tree or plant may be benefitted. My aim is to fix on the mind of the reader that when you are sick and you call in a physician, you ask him if he can cure you. If he says, yes, and prescribes quinine, you don't ask him what there is in quinine that perfects the cure. Nevertheless it may become necessary, in some instances in my case to have to go so far as to explain this. You take for instance barn-yard manure. About all the good derived from this kind of manure is the ammonia that it contains. The farmers quite frequently pile the manure up in heaps and let it stand till it heats, then it begins to smoke so that a stranger passing by early in the morning would almost have sworn that he had just passed an ammonia manufactory and that all the tanks had bursted. It would have been much better to put the manure under the ground where it belongs before it had lost its strength.

One time in Canada I told an Irishman that his trees needed mulching. No sooner said than done. He piled up about half a load around the stock of every tree. The consequence was the manure heated and he killed a few and hurt them all. The next time I met this gentleman, had it not been that he was a devoted Christian, the only thing that would have saved me from a good sound hammering would have been my legs, as the Irish don't do this kind of thing on the halves usually. Dig the manure into the ground, plow it under, scatter it broadcast, but don't pile it up in heaps around the stock. If you do, dig it away forming something similar to a hen's nest around the base. There are other manures that I must not let go unnoticed, chip manure for instance. Clean up your chip-yards; scatter this around the trees at the base, as chip manure won't heat. Don't throw out your soap-suds, as it would make a fine nourishing drink at the roots of some ailing tree.

I will conclude this subject by making a few assertions. I will take a Bartlett pear tree. Suppose this tree produces an inferior quality of fruit of its kind. Let me say, if a chemist will tell me what the fruit lacks in its natural flavor and that flavor comes from the ground, I can reproduce that flavor. If it is lime it wants I can feed it lime; if ammonia, I can feed it ammonia; if it is nitrogen or phosphatic acid it needs, this it will get by the use of bone-meal or otherwise. I don't care if this trouble comes from some atmospheric cause, I can produce the desired effect. Certain trees need certain food. Suppose you plant an orchard where the land is particularly adapted to the growing of fruit and fruit trees. Is it not reasonable to suppose that after many years of heavy bearing that this orchard has exhausted the natural food in nature's storehouse? I think it is, and that food should be again supplied artificially by the horticulturist who has received the benefit of his fruitful orchard.

THE INSECTICIDE.

There are many reasons why the "Prof. Brown's Insecticide" is the best.

1st. It is a compound, compounded from all the best known insecticides known to the world.

2nd. It is so scientifically compounded that when manufactured according to the formula, there is no visible separation of the many chemicals which go to form a part of this compound.

3rd. Being composed of the best insecticides, it has the advantage over others, from the fact that what will kill one insect will not kill another. Kerosene oil emulsion is considered one of the very best insecticides for the extermination of sap-sucking insects. Admitting this to be a fact, it is hard to mix oil and water without separating, the oil rising to the top. There is at least four gallons of kerosene oil used to 100 lbs. of the "Brown Insecticide", with no separation.

4th. Tobacco is another insecticide, one of the very best known, but it fails to kill all kinds of insects. Tobacco will kill some species of insects and will not kill another; this can be proven from the fact that the tobacco worm and grass-hopper will live and get fat on the tobacco plant. Nevertheless tobacco as an insecticide is like whiskey, good in its place. And I have found its place by making it a part of my compound. Whale oil soap is another one of the very best known insecticides, and I believe it to be used as extensively as any. Nevertheless it won't kill the codlin moth. Whale oil soap as an exterminator stands high in my estimation, from the fact that it is made from the carbon of potash and fish oil and this forms the solid in "Browns Insect Exterminator." Sulphur mixed with powder and lard will cure the seven year itch (para siate), but put this on vegetation in this form and it is too penetrating. When put into a soap I consider it one of the best. Therefore if it is sulphur you want, you will find it in the "Brown's Insecticide." Carbolic acid is a fine insecticide when properly used. It is a part of the "Brown's Insect Exterminator." These with three more equally as good, are the insecticides of which the "Prof. Brown's Insecticide" is composed of.

Anyone who knows anything about insecticides, knows that if the medicines herein referred to are what goes to make up the above named compound, and if so compounded as to cause no separation, it must be acknowledged to be the best because it is so compounded as to kill all kinds of insects. I have spent hundreds of dollars in perfecting this compound so as to make it what it is, without question, the best compound of its kind that has ever been invented, and when used once will be used again. One more good quality this medicine has, it is not only an insect exterminator, but one of the best fertilizers. Any one who knows anything about this subject knows that lye is good, soap suds are good, also tobacco. My whole study has been to use nothing in this compound that would not be beneficial to vegetation as well as an insect destroyer.

WHAT IS CLAIMED FOR IT.

This Insecticide, if prepared and used according to directions, is warranted to kill the San Jose Scale, the Oyster Shell Scale, the Woolly Aphis, the Green Aphis, the Plum Aphis, the Hop Aphis, the Cherry and Pear Tree Slug, Caterpillars, and in fact all insects injurious to trees, shrubs, plants, vines and their foliage.

An orchard infested by any of the above, especially the San Jose Scale, or Woolly Aphis, cannot be cleaned and kept free from them by one spraying, but should be treated within a month to a second spraying to kill any that may not have been reached the first time, and then should be sprayed twice each year as a preventive measure.

To secure the best results, good, thorough work must be done. Large trees should be well cut back and all loose bark scraped off, being careful to burn all limbs and bark thus removed. The earth should be removed from about the base of the tree, exposing the larger roots of those infested with the Woolly Aphis, and a few shovelfuls of lime or strong wood ashes placed about the base of the tree; then thoroughly drench with the liquid as used for spraying and replace the earth; after which place another shovelful of lime or ashes about the base of the tree. This will prevent the Aphis that infest the roots from working up the body of the tree, which they will if nothing is done to prevent them.

SPRAYING.

The method of reaching the insects with "Brown's Insect Exterminator," is by one of the numerous inexpensive machines invented for the purpose. Small hand force pumps are generally used, where there are but few trees and vines, but larger machines are required for hopfields and orchards. The operation of spraying is quite simple, inexpensive and very effective. The use of the "Insect Exterminator" will double or quadruple the income from orchards that have been devastated by insect pests. Evening is regarded as the best time to apply the Exterminator, as it is less liable to evaporate, and longer time is given it to take effect upon the pests.

The season for spraying fruit trees for codlin moth is when the blossoms are falling, the calyx end of the young fruit then presenting a saucer-like depression for receiving and holding the fluid, and as it is at this end of the fruit that the insects begin their work, it is the first place they will be compelled to take their fatal medicine.

PROF. BROWN'S FAVORITE PRESCRIPTION.

I have shown to the best of my ability, in previous articles, that insects of a pestiferous nature have waged war on the fruit industry of our country, and being aware that many of our most eminent divines and physicians, and also some of our ablest statesmen, have their favorite prescription, which they often prescribe to make their profession a success; in fact the Savior of this world seems to me not exempt from such a prescription.

Did he not say to the men who accused the woman of adultery, "Those of you who have no sin, cast the first stone"? Did he not say to the self-righteous, "Thou hypocrite, cast out the beam out of thine own eye so that thou canst see more clearly to cast the mote out of thy brother's eye"? Is it not a fact that the Savior said, "If the fountain head be corrupt, the whole stream is, or will become as poisonous"?

While the writer of this article is unlike the Savior of the world in many respects, nevertheless I have my favorite prescription. The capital of the United States is the fountain head of this government. There is the place where the laws are enacted that go to govern the welfare of this nation. It is long since the law-makers of this nation saw the approaching danger and calamity the insect foe was about to bring to this country. The speedy action on the part of our law-makers in formulating and enacting laws to get rid as well as to keep rid of this foe, deserves great credit. Through this means it soon became the duty of the Commissioner of Agriculture to have a department of Entomology connected with his department. Some of the most eminent men have set about to devise ways and means to assist in this work of extermination. These gentlemen advised the enactment of laws that would prohibit infested products from foreign countries being shipped into this. This advice was favorably considered by Congress and stringent laws were passed. Soon this question became so important that it has been carried into one state legislature then another till about every state in the Union has fallen into line. State boards have been appointed whose duty it is to see that the laws are enforced, one of which is, "clean up your trees, if infested, or we will cut them down." Experimental stations have been established in horticultural colleges in almost every state in the Union, and vast sums of money are paid out annually by both state and national governments to devise ways and means to get rid of this calamity.

Is it not a fact that the fountain is impure, from the fact that many of the cities where experimental stations exist are badly infested with insect pests which seem to be increasing every year? Is it not a fact that while some members of the state boards are out lecturing in remote parts of their state and showing how to clean up orchards, that in the immediate vicinity where such officers reside, orchards are crawling alive with noxious insects? In many of our capital cities, the fountain head of our governments, from whence these laws were enacted, the fruit, shade and ornamental trees are being destroyed almost within the shadow of the capitol building. It is a fact, and why is it? Is it because our wise legislatures have failed to pass a law that can be enforced by the strong arm of the law? Is it because they failed to make an appropriation sufficient to enforce those laws, or is it not because there are men that are opposed to the enforcement of the law? The officers have known this to be a fact, and in consequence when they come in contact with such men, they simply shut their eyes to the existence of the infested orchards and pass them by unnoticed. Whole cities are in the same condition. I don't say this is the case in all states. California is an exception, as the fruit growers of that great fruit-growing commonwealth have long since opened their eyes to the fact that something had to be done and they are doing it.

Now let me ask, is there any infested fruit in Washington City, D. C., any red scale on oranges, lemon scale on lemons, San Jose scale on apples or apple trees? If so, as that city is the great fountain-head of this great government, commence there at once and don't stop until the very letter of the law is put into effect. Let the fountain-head of this nation be pure and then let this purity of purpose as well as action spread its angelic wings of purity over every capital city in this beloved land of ours. Then let the officers of the law go forth with a decree: "Clean up your orchards and vineyards or the law will clean them up for you." At the same time don't lose sight of the importance of cleaning up your own orchards before you exact your neighbor to clean up his, as "consistency thou art a jewel." Let this decree go forth and be carried out in the strictest letter of the law, until every orchard and vineyard will be found a spring of purity, casting its waters into the many tributaries that flow into the many great rivers that go to form the many fountains that majestically flow into the one great fountain which has become the head of this nation.

I have given to the readers of this chapter the true formula of my prescription, and my only hope is that it may be read by the many who have this important subject at heart, and that it may have the effect desired by its author.

TREATMENT OF OLD TREES.

If the trees are old, cut off all cross and top limbs and surplus branches, scrape off all the rough bark. After this is done, take hot grafting wax composed of the following material and apply it to all cuts and wounds: One pound of tallow, two pounds of rosin and one pound of beeswax, melt and put on the wounds and cuts with a paint brush. This work should be done in the fall, winter or spring, while the trees are dormant. Dig around the trees to a depth of 12 or 18 inches, care being taken to not mutilate the roots. Take half a bushel of well rotted manure (hen manure being preferable), two shovelsful of air-slaked lime, also two of bone meal, then mix the manure, earth and lime thoroughly and place the same around the roots; then saturate the ground with the Insect Exterminator.

After this has been done in the spring before the leaves are out, dissolve the Exterminator at the rate of one pound to five gallons of hot water and stir well until thoroughly mixed, then add three gallons of cold, soft water, and apply the same.

NO BLACK-HEARTED TREES IN MY GRANDFATHER'S ORCHARD.

Black-hearted tree and the cause, is one of the many subjects I am often called on to explain, and of course I am expected to answer any and all questions pertaining to my profession. Nevertheless I am frank to confess that it is one of the numerous questions that has a tendency to baffle the wisest theorist who has given it the deepest thought. My aim in life is and always has been to study the questions that I consider worthy of my consideration, both from a practical and a theoretical standpoint. When I was a boy in Canada, or in fact in New York state, a black-hearted tree was a scarcity. Now they are to be found in almost all of the finest orchards of our nation. Are my assertions correct? Am I right or wrong? If right, why is it? It can't be the climate that has produced this change. Some say it is, I say it is not. I can show you orchards that have stood for 70 years and are mostly healthy trees to this day; and I can show you orchards that are only 10 or 15 years old that have but few sound trees in them. Some have black hearts and some have something else. Now let us sit down and in all candor diagnose this case.

After a thorough investigation we find a young man, about 70 years ago, felling the trees in the state of Ohio, Michigan, or perhaps other of the Eastern States, with one object in view, and one alone, that being to make a home for himself and the one who had consented to share life's pleasures with him.

Tree by tree slowly but surely succumbs to the woodman's axe. Now the place where stood two years ago a part of the mammoth forest, stand 10 broad acres of treeless landscape, dotted with stumps like stars in the starry heavens. Fastened to mother earth, they sit seemingly bidding defiance to the further progress of the brawny woodman, he not yet having learned the meaning of the word fail. Stump after stump disappeared as their smoke went up, telling the story that even the giant of the forest yielded submission to the will of man.

This being accomplished, soon the bachelor's hall was made the happy home of the young bride, who had so kindly consented to tread life's pathway with him. A sub-division of this 10 acres was soon made for corn and grain, the balance set aside for a permanent garden and orchard. But how to succeed best in this new enterprise was as yet a question to be solved. Looking over the many treasures stowed away in the young bride's trunk, an old-fashioned pocket was found, containing perhaps a peck of apple seeds, plum pits, peach and other precious seed, placed there by the hand of a loving father, or perhaps dampened by the tears of a fond mother as she carefully stowed them away with many other treasures of a similar nature. Soon the seeds are sown, and what a conglomerated mass, as they had been selected from perhaps 50 seedlings of apple, plum, peach and cherry mixed and sown in the same nursery rows, with no two seeds, perhaps, alike when taken from the same apple. Nevertheless these seeds were perfect, as they were perfect specimens of nature's offspring (no adulteration). Soon spring came and almost with supernatural perfection an infant tree sprang into existence from every seed that had been sown, hoed, pruned and cultivated.

Two years soon passed when these young seedlings were removed to their place of destination. In a short time these trees came into general bearing, and what a sight to behold! The trees natural beauties. The apples all sizes from the wild crab to the 20 oz. pippin, and all the colors of the rainbow, were nowhere to be compared with what was to be found in this young orchard. Some were sweet, some sour, some good, some bad, as far as the fruit was concerned; but so far as the trees were concerned they could not be described by anything but perfection itself. Therefore the foundation was good. The owner seeing that something must be done in the way of grafting into the natural stock in order to obtain a superior grade of fruit, soon most of the natural branches had been removed, being replaced with a first class quality of fruit, such as Northern Spy, Rhode Island Greening, Golden Russet, Bell Flower and many others too numerous to mention. Therefore a wonderful change has been wrought. I have seen thirteen varieties of delicious apples growing on one tree, making good the words of our Lord when he said, "I am the true vine, ye are the branches."

But what a wonderful change has taken place. The wilderness has disappeared and what once was a dense forest is now a great commonwealth. The sowing of the fruit seed in the garden, in order to grow an orchard, is a thing of the past. Large commercial nurseries have taken the place of that custom. The grafting into the limbs of trees is almost a thing that once was but is no more. The hardy seedling stock has obtained a substitute by grafting a tender stock into a hardy root. This system has proved a success in many instances, but as a rule I am of the opinion that more ruin has come to our orchards from this one practice than from all others combined. In fact, I have investigated this practice so I am convinced that 95 per cent. of all black-hearted trees are attributed to this one cause. Therefore I would say, although a great lover of science for the good of the orchard, give us, in this case, more nature and less science.

TWIG BLIGHT.

This is one of the many subjects which seem to baffle the skill of the most skillful physicians of trees at the present time, to be found in our nation. There being a great diversity of opinion as to the true origin of the cause, the question as to the cause is of little importance to the orchardist. It may be to scientists, it cannot be otherwise. Can it be cured, is the question, and if so, how? The fact it can be cured is no longer a question in my mind. Read the following from the *Colorado Field and Farm*, of Sept. 14, 1893:

"The science of tree doctoring may in time become a recognized occupation among horticulturists. Professor Brown, of Seattle, Washington, is in the business exclusively, and during a visit to Denver last April he applied some remedial measures to a Wealthly apple tree in the orchard of David Brothers on Wheat Ridge. This tree was nearly dead from three years attack of blight. To-day it is thrifty and apparently recovered from its recent illness. Its new growth of twigs measures over two feet and the tree is saved, whereas it would surely have been dead by this time but for Dr. Brown's treatment."

But, says the critic, any one can get any kind of a testimonial in a paper if he pays for it. Admitting that to be perhaps a fact, I have this to say: I have never seen this tree since I operated on it, I never heard of the patient until I received three papers, one from Colorado, one from Iowa and one from Ill. I must say with due courtesy to these editors, I have never acknowledged the receipt of those favors. I was somewhat surprised at its marvelous growth and it would not surprise me if the tree had died.

The first thing I did to this tree was to give it a good pruning, the next was to give it a good washing, so as to open the pores. Then my aim was to find what kind of sap flowed in its veins, pure or impure. I examined the lungs, (the leaves), to see if the breathing apparatus was all right, then I went to the roots to see if they were too far gone to partake of nourishment and medicine. I found a very sick patient. I prescribed a stimulant, also a blood purifier and an insect exterminator. The result was I cured my patient, but like many other patients it got well perhaps a little too fast. It produced a two feet growth. If this tree was permitted to go into winter with those tender growths, that should have been cut back almost a foot, in Sept., so as to harden the wood for winter, besides having its roots well mulched, the tree might die. Be that as it may, I cured the tree, and if the nurse had let it overdo itself so as to cause a relapse, it would be his fault and not mine. I have this to say for the nurse, Mr. David Brothers, he is a gentleman and his wife a lady. I found the blight bringing ruin to many orchards in Colorado, some being completely ruined.

I went from Denver to Salt Lake and found that this disease had put in its appearance, but to no great extent; went from Salt Lake to Boise City, Idaho, and found it a little worse in Idaho than in Utah. Returned home so as to spend the 4th with my family.

Having been informed that the blight was doing great damage in Iowa and Nebraska, I left Seattle the 15th day of August, by way of the Great Northern to St. Paul, and by Minneapolis to Council Bluffs, Iowa. This city and vicinity has long been noted for its fine apples, and now what can be said? I don't mean to exaggerate in a single instance, neither do I when I say the apple trees of Council Bluffs are a pitiable sight to behold. Hundreds of trees are dead and many more dying. After a stay of only one and one-half days, I took train for Fremont, Neb. While I found many blighted trees in this city, they were not near as bad as at Council Bluffs. Making but a short stay, I took train for Lincoln. Finding the condition much the same, I hastened to Bennett, 18 miles from Lincoln, having lived in this locality for over three years, while a commercial man for Bloomington nurseries, and having sold more trees in that part during the years of '78, '79 and '80 than all the other tree salesmen put together. I found hundreds of fine large orchards that had been sold by me as little two or three year olds, had now become mammoth fruit trees, but I am sorry to say that on a further examination I found that many of those orchards had, to all appearances, been stung by the sting of death. While I found but few trees dead, very many were dying. I staid with my old time friends and acquaintances for over two months. I found that some of the orchardists had given up all hope, while others were satisfied that their orchards could be saved, and are putting forth an effort to save them, using my prescription. I am sorry to say that this writing is too early in the season to know what success will crown their efforts. As I stated before, there seems to be such a diversity of opinion as to the cause, nevertheless I find two to one who believe that this blight is caused by the hot sun, while others say it is electricity. I differ; I claim that it is beyond any question a parasite, and must be treated as such. Others say it can't be cured, I say it can; I say if it can't be cured, it means ruin to the apple and pear industry in the United States.

TREATMENT.

Use same method as for Peach Yellow.

TOMATO BLIGHT.

During July and August, 1892, I made a trip from Seattle to Eastern Washington and Idaho, stopping at Ellensburg and Spokane, Wash., thence to Moscow, Idaho, thence by stage to Lewiston, thence by row boat down the Snake River (75 miles) to Rapera, thence to Walla Walla. On my return trip I stopped at Grant, The Dalles, thence to Seattle by way of Portland, Ore. My only object in making this trip was to investigate what diseases were to be found in the orchard and vegetable kingdom. In my line of travel I found that both orchard and garden had fallen heir to many diseases, such as San Jose scale, woolly aphis, codlin moth and many others of a similar nature. But what I found to an alarming extent was tomato blight, this being the finest tomato producing country I ever saw. I found that whole acres had been planted. The crop looked thrifty and fine, when all at once the tops began to turn yellow. This, following down the stalks, soon reached the roots and the crop became a dismal failure. I find that some writers on this subject advise the planting of crops in the shade or putting a roof of muslin over the broad acres devoted to this industry in this state and elsewhere. Let me ask, is it not the same climate, sun, heat and moisture those people have now that they had when they grew mammoth crops for many years previous to the arrival of this dreadful disease? Then if it is, why raise a perfect crop then, and blighted crop now? Permit me to answer this question. Years ago you had no disease in your tomato crop, now you have tomato cholera (blight). This disease, without a question in my mind, is a vegetable parasite and has been sent to us by seed or otherwise, and like the cholera in the human family, it is transmitted to the sap through the pores, making its death mission seen and felt on the most tender branches, growing worse and worse till the sting of death has performed its mission.

The remedy that I would advise: Never plant your tomatoes in the same place two years in succession. Never plant seed grown from infested plants. Don't plant your seed in the same hot bed without first removing all old earth that has been used the previous year. Fumigate hot beds thoroughly with burning sulphur, then whitewash with lime. When you plant the seed, soak over night in No. 10 or some other good insecticide. When you set out your plants put a little lime and guano, also bone meal, in the earth that you plant them in. A tablespoon full of guano is enough for a six quart pan of earth. Scatter lime broadcast over your field so as to make the ground look white. Spray often with No. 10, as for green aphis. (I don't say that this treatment will cure, but I am of the opinion that it will. Investigate by following my directions and see for yourself.)

PEACH YELLOW.

This is a subject that has been agitating the minds of many horticulturists, who have been and are interested in the growing of this delicious fruit. Well it may be, from the fact that it is and has been laying waste, to a very great extent, the peach growing industry of many of the Eastern and Southern states, and is commencing to put in its appearance west of the Rocky Mountains, having been found to exist in many fine young orchards in the vicinity of Salt Lake, Utah; one orchard in particular, owned by a Mr. King. This gentleman has about 15 acres of fine bearing trees, but sad to say, Mr. King purchased a bill of trees from an Eastern firm, and with this order came the peach yellow. I examined the young orchard while in Utah, this (1894) spring and am sorry to say I found about 25 trees dead from this cause, and perhaps 150 in a dying condition. In fact the disease is scattered broadcast over the orchard. This disease I found to exist both in Oregon and Washington, in the great peach growing belts of the Columbia and Snake river valleys.

It is not so much a question that it does exist as how to get rid of it. I am often asked the question, Can the peach yellow be cured? My answer is most emphatically, yes. In answering in the affirmative, I am aware of the fact that I am brought to differ greatly from many prominent theorists and practical horticulturists. Nevertheless doctors differ as regards the curing of diseases in the human family, why not horticulturists differ? Has any professor wrought any more marvelous changes or cures in his profession than has the horticulturist? From the poisonous peach almond they have produced the most wholesome and delicious fruit ever made use of by man. I am aware that both professions have their quacks, and I am of the opinion that the horticulturist profession has more than its share. All I ask of those who may criticise the curing of this disease is to investigate what are the component parts of the medicine and the method by which the cure is performed. Give it a thorough test and judge for themselves.

FALL OR WINTER TREATMENT FOR PEACH YELLOW.

The first thing to be done is to trim back to the living wood. Don't make a cut where you have not cut into the living wood cut the top back pretty well and scrape all the rough bark off the tree. Then spray with arsenical compound at the rate of 1 lb. to 8 or 10 gals. of water. Put in enough lime to make the trees take on a creamy cast. Put hot grafting wax on all of the wounds caused by trimming or otherwise. Spray with this treatment after the leaves have fallen and again just as the buds begin to get large in the spring; again immediately after the blossoms have fallen, and again ten days from date of last spraying; then again in 15 days. Treat the roots with the same treatment as for apple twig blight. Don't forget this part of it or your trees will not be cured.

BLACK SPOT.

I have found in my travels, that this insect is doing considerable damage to apple and pear orchards in almost all of the central and middle states, reaching west and south as far as California, doing great damage to some varieties of trees, seemingly more to young trees, than those of more mature age. The first thing that becomes noticeable is a little sunken spot in the bark, having a dark brown appearance, finally becoming black, the spots varying in size from a ten cent piece to that of a saucer (sometimes larger). The second year the bark mostly separates from the wood. I have examined the bark to see if I could find any perforation, but failed to find any whatever. I have then removed the bark, placed it under a microscope and almost invariably found a large quantity of active, little parasites. How they got there is a mystery; I can't say that I really know, but there is one thing certain, they are there, and that they are of the *Phyloxera* family. I don't consider this a hard disease to cure if taken in time. I make this statement from the fact that I have treated bad cases of this disease in some fifteen different states; my first in Michigan, my last in California. Let me be right or wrong as regards the true cause of this disease, the one important question is "can it be cured," and if so, how? I answer this question by giving my prescription, being one I have prescribed for years and I can say at the present writing, I have never lost a tree where my prescription was properly administered.

DIRECTIONS.

First thing to be done is to remove all the affected bark, scrape the wood so as to take all decayed substance off the wood. Cut into the live bark so as when done you have a fresh wound all around the affected part. Then apply hot grafting wax with a brush (put grafting wax on hot). If the affected place is large, cover the wound over with a piece of muslin which will adhere to the grafting wax, then paint the muslin with the same prescription. If the tree is old, fertilize so as to start the tree growing. Use same treatment as for peach yellows. If the tree is very bad I always protect it by the use of a board (see "Planting an Orchard"), as described in a previous article.

GRASS HOPPERS.

It was in the spring of 1868, that I accepted of Horace Greeley's advice: "Go west, young man, go west." Having accumulated considerable of this world's goods, I hitched a fine pair of blacks to my carriage and started on an overland trip from Chicago, on the first day of Sept. of the same year, enroute for southern Minnesota. I arrived about Oct. first and located at Graham Lake in Nobles county, and, like many other young men, I was very anxious to become a land owner in the then far west. I soon lay claim to 160 acres as a soldiers' homestead. Soon a pre-emption, then a tree claim; after which I added to my possessions by buying more from the railroad company. My main object was to soon become the greatest nursery-man on earth. I soon had men and teams at work erecting a shanty. April soon came and I had teams at work rolling over the sod; then wheat was being sowed on the new breaking broadcast; harvest came, and strange to say 12 bushels of No. 1 wheat per acre came with it. I imagine how I must have looked as I stood with my arms folded, viewing my possessions, and how I figured to add more to my landed estate. Soon the fall plowing was done, winter passed and spring was with us; 50 acres of wheat was then sowed, with other crops in accordance. Imagine how I must have felt when old wheat prophets informed me that I had a good prospect for an average wheat crop of 45 to 50 bushels per acre, and all the rest of my crops with much the same prospects. But after dinner, one beautiful mid-summer day, just about the time the wheat was in the dough, I stood in the door viewing my possessions and was about to exclaim, "I am monarch of all I survey, my rights there are none to dispute," when I saw something like a snowflake fall in the wheat, then another, and casting my eyes heavenward, looking the sun square in the face, I found that the sun was somewhat darkened by something that had the appearance of a snow storm. Soon the storm had fallen, and the sun shone with renewed brightness. But what a sight to see; every stalk of grain was laid level with the ground, the weight of the grasshoppers being so great. In 48 hours the crop was so far ruined that I only thrashed 35 bushels of inferior wheat that year; their mission was accomplished, as far as the destruction of the crop was concerned; but there was more to follow. The first day seemed to be devoted to the destruction of vegetation; the second to co-habiting; and the third to boring holes in the ground, and the depositing of eggs for a second crop. It was interesting to anyone who was given to the study of nature to have watched the scientific process by which the egg deposit was conducted. The first thing they did was to bore with their tail's end into the ground, as far as they could get for their wings. This when completed was as smoothly and scientifically done as if bored with a gimblet. After this work has been performed the next work was to line the inside of the hole with a kind of glue-wax, which when done had somewhat the appearence of a honey cell. Then commenced the egg deposit; every hole was filled with eggs averaging from 75 to 100 each. After this work was done the next thing they did was to cap the cell with the same substance that they built the walls of the cell of; after which they covered the cell over with the loose dirt that they had excavated to make the hole with. This was done to hide their deposit from their enemies. It froze 40 degrees below zero that winter, and some hoped that the eggs would be killed by the frost. Every one sowed in the spring; soon the eggs hatched and the young hoppers appeared as numerous as the sands of the sea shore. This work of destruction they persisted in for four years, and by this time I left my possessions to grasshoppers and creditors, wending my way with my wife to St. Paul and at the same time swearing vengence on grasshoppers.

I can assure the readers of this sketch that to this day I can't look into the face of a grasshopper with the least degree of allowance; and as for me to try to give a concise history of what further happened, I would say "write a book."

REMEDY.

When you see them in the air like a snow storm, fix your eyes on them until you see them begin to alight. When you have made sure that they have lit, if you are a fiddler, you must commence playing the "Arkansas Traveler" and never let up until you see them arise and take their flight. Then you must change your tune by substituting, "Let old acquaintance be forgot and never brought to mind," and keep this up until you have seen the last of this particular swarm. Then see if they have deposited their eggs. If they have, burn off your grain fields (that is if you do not want the straw) then do no fall plowing, but keep up one continual dragging so as to let birds and ants have free access to them. If they hatch thick in the spring, sow no small grain, but dig a deep ditch around five acres so as to be ready when they commence to travel, to strew straw in the ditch so that when they fall in you can burn them up. Don't plow the five acres that you have reserved until late in the spring. Add arsenical compound to No. 14 and spray before plowing; then plow, plant and spray, and by keeping this up may get a part of a crop.

THE FRUITS OF BOISE BASIN.

Boise Basin, in which is situated Boise City, the capital of Idaho, has long been regarded as the garden spot of Idaho. It is possessed of rich soil that produces everything found in the temperate zone, and its climate is unsurpassed, being equible and healthful. The season in this basin or valley, is somewhat earlier than in the far-famed Salt Lake Valley, by reason of the lesser altitude, and crops mature earlier than in Salt Lake Valley. Horticulturists who have visited Boise Basin with a view to permanent location, pronounce it one of the best fruit sections of the United States, but at the same time they state that it is the most pest-infected portion of the Rocky Mountains, Salt Lake not excepted. Once noted for its superior fruit, it is now afflicted with infected orchards, its myriads of codlin moth, aphis and other fruit-destroying insects. The trees are literally alive with these insects which have taken the place of the beautiful and luscious fruit once so prolific in this beautiful country. The orchards, once a source of great profit to the horticulturist, are at present quite the reverse of this and their glory is departing. How to recupe the trees, is the question now confronting the orchardists of Boise. Can they be restored to their former vigor and be made as prolific and profitable as in their earlier years? is the question. They undoubtedly can, but the owners of these splendid orchards cannot restore them by standing around with their hands in their pockets. It is going to require work to accomplish this end, and the sooner it is undertaken, the more quickly it will be accomplished. The work of restoration should no longer be delayed, and it should be pushed energetically and persistently. It means a great deal to Boise and to the state of Idaho. It means the restoration of confidence in Idaho as a great fruit growing state; it means additional wealth to the community.

BARK BOUND TREES.

Leaves being the lungs of the trees, they sometimes fail to do their duty, and as a result there is an overflow of sap which fails to reach its destination and therefore comes to instantaneous standstill, bursts nature's blood vessels and the tree bleeds. This causes the tree to be bark-bound. In this case take a sharp knife and cut the bark, commencing on the large limbs and down to the large brace roots, cutting back to the wood. This should be followed by same prescription as mentioned for borers.

FUNGUS DISEASES.

There is and has been much said regarding this disease among fruit growers generally. And well there may be, from the fact that a great portion of the apple crop of this part of the coast has been ruined this year (1894) by this disease. I find but few of the fruit growers whom I have interviewed have much idea what it is or what they have to contend with. They know they have it, and many are battling against this disease. One gentleman who resides at Ross, Washington, has sprayed twice with a highly recommended insecticide, which has proved a failure. The orchardist should be educated so as to realize the fact that this disease is a vegetable parasitical fungus, and is in its nature like smut on wheat. The wheat may lay in a granary all winter, the germ of the disease dried with the wheat, so it is hard to realize how the germ of life in either could exist. Nevertheless when sown they both spring into life. So it is with the apple and pear fungus. The live fungus germ is to be found on the tree in the winter. It will be found on the dead leaves under the trees, and when I have been searching for this species in the orchards I have often hummed to myself, "The old oaken bucket, the moss covered bucket," etc. The time to get rid of smut on wheat is before it is sown. The time to get rid of or lessen apple or pear scab, is to trim, spray and clean your orchards while in a dormant condition. Kill the germ and you kill the life. Don't wait until the horse is stolen before you lock the stable door.

A RECENT VISIT TO SOME OF THE HOP FIELDS OF WASHINGTON.

Having been informed of the great damage and partial ruin the hop aphis had brought to the hop crop of 1893 in the state of Washington, I concluded to make another visit in order to see if I could ascertain what might be looked for in the way of another invasion of this pest the present year. I arrived home on or about the first day of May from an extensive trip in Utah, as mentioned in a previous article, and I immediately commenced an investigation of this subject. There being many hop vines planted for ornament in many of the yards of this city (Seattle), I was not at a loss to find the object of my purpose, and that was to satisfy myself whether or not the hop aphis was going to put in an appearance. Day after day my glass was brought to bear on the hop leaves in many yards of this city. On the 10th day of May I found the great object of my prolonged search, and that was one solitary hop fly in the act of depositing her eggs. On a close and still closer observation I found in the lapse of three days that one hundred had come as reinforcements. This being the case, on or about June 1st I set out for a visit to the hop fields, making my first stop at Kent, a beautiful little city situated 16 miles south of Seattle, and in the midst of the great hop growing belt of the famous White River valley. I soon met one of the most prominent hop growers, who was no less than Senator Vandevanter. When informed of my mission he took me into his buggy and I accompanied him to his large hop yard which was not far distant. On my arrival in the hop field, in the first hill I found lice in small numbers, and in the next and so on. I soon satisfied my curiosity, much to the disgust of the owner of this beautiful hop ranch.

On my return to Kent, I set out for another ranch just south of the city. With grip in hand I had only gone a short distance when I met a gentleman who immediately seemed to look me up one side and down the other, seemingly trying to determine in his own mind whether I was or was not a stray from Coxey's army (this army having just left Seattle). After passing the usual salutations, I ventured to ask, "Are you a hop-grower, sir?" "Yes, sir?" was the prompt reply. Being then in close proximity to a hop field, he with the point of the finger and the nod of the head, informed me that he was the owner. Becoming somewhat nervous from my imaginary idea of who this gentleman took me to be, I thoughtlessly continued, "Are you lousy, sir?" With one fierce look that would have made an army mule shake like an aspen leaf, he advanced three paces toward me. I unhesitatingly moved my forces three paces to the rear. "What do you mean, sir," was his reply, "do you mean to insult me?" "No-o sir," was my speedy answer, in a trembling voice, "it is the hop lice I mean, sir." A pleasant smile came over the gentleman's face when I explained my mission to the hop fields of White River Valley. After a pleasant hand-shake and due apologies were exchanged, I immediately became the guest of my newly-made friend. He escorted me to his residence, whereupon his estimable wife finding that I was much in need of what is always essential to supply the wants of the inner man, set about to supply the long-felt want. After a sumptuous repast, I was conducted to his hop ranch, where I immediately commenced the search, but was not long in determining satisfactorily to my own mind, that the pest was to be found in this yard (in small numbers) from center to circumference. Having satisfied myself of this fact, I was soon on the road.

Being somewhat acquainted with one of Washington's hop-kings, who lived about five miles distant, I started out with grip in hand. Passing one hop field after another I soon reached my destination. I was ushered into the presence of his majesty, who was no less a personage than Mr. Patrick Hayes, who is the first, it is said who ventured to plant a hop ranch in Washington, and who is now one of the many who have made hop growing a grand success, in the greatest hop producing country on this continent (in my opinion). After a pleasant greeting by Mr. Hayes and his genial and much esteemed wife and family, the evening was not long in passing. Thereupon I was shown by my host to my final resting place for the night. After first viewing my pleasant surroundings, my weary body was soon at rest and sound asleep in a bed good enough for the king himself.

In the morning after being shown through one of his mammoth hop fields, I became convinced that the hop aphis was no respecter of persons. Being persuaded of this fact, I also was convinced of another in my own mind, that is if the hop crop of Washington is saved in 1894, it will only be by one persistent effort on the part of the hop growers in the way of spraying, and even then, I am of the opinion, in spite of their efforts, they will not be able to save more than a two-thirds crop. Something will have to be done more than has ever been in the way of a general cleaning up of the orchards, in order to destroy the egg deposit. Had I a hop ranch and an orchard, I would see to it that there was not a living insect germ left in it. I would cut down all wild plum and brush that was near the hop field; burn all old vines and clean up generally. As this is a very important part to be taken in this war of extermination, as I have said before, let me say again, I would rather undertake to destroy a thousand insects while in a dormant condition, or in egg form, than to destroy 10 while winged and flying in the air. The sooner the farmers become educated, and have opened their eyes to this fact, the sooner they will have waged a successful war against their common enemy. After cleaning up, they should spray with salt, sulphur and lime. Saturate the ground well, drenching the hills, and spray again as early as the young shoots begin to appear; then keep up one continual spraying until the crop is safe. The worst trouble that I see is the expense of the medicine they now use (quassia and whale oil soap). If the hop growers can't get a cure that is cheaper than soap and quassia, the cost will greatly lessen the profits.

A NEW ENEMY OF WASHINGTON HOPS.

Soon after returning from my visit to the hop fields, described in the preceding article, I was informed that a new disease had been discovered in a hop yard in the Puyallup valley, a distance of 36 miles from Seattle. This being somewhat in my line of investigation I was soon en route for the scene of action. I had not traveled over eight miles when I began to enter and pass through some of the hop fields to be found in my line of march, the fields becoming larger, still larger, as they presented themselves to my view, until they seemed to form one great city of stakes, covering an area of thousands of acres. I can asure the readers of this narrative, it was a sight to behold, from the fact that the vines had reached the top of the poles, presenting an appearance as though planted there for ornament, each four hills forming a perfect square, the poles being in straight lines each way; these poles were about ten feet high and great care seemed to have been observed in getting them all the same height. Commencing at one corner of these great fields, to the corner stake was fastened a strong twine, held seemingly by a nail in the top of the pole. This twine was stretched and fastened, both ways, over nearly all the hop fields that came to my notice, forming one great network of twine. The hop vine having reached the top of the poles, had sent out millions of runners, which, fastening themselves to the twine soon formed one majestic roof over the entire hop fields, regardless of size.

My mind having been absorbed in wonderment, time soon passed, and the day was far spent. After passing between two great hop fields, there came to my notice that beautiful little city (Puyallup,) that is known not only in every state of this Union, but in every civilized nation on earth, as being the greatest hop shipping city in the world for its size.

Having one great object in view, on my arrival I hastened to learn where this newly discovered disease was to be found, and was informed that it was discovered in one of Mr. Meeker's large fields just east of the city. I asked, what Meeker? Ezra Meeker, was the prompt reply. With grip in hand I immediately went to Mr. Meeker's office. I was informed that he was not in, but was expected every minute. Making the object of my visit known to the gentlemen who were in charge of the office, one of them kindly offered to accompany me to the hop field where the disease was located. His offer was accepted, and I soon found myself in a hop field containing, I presume, 75 acres. I was not long in discovering the fact that the disease was not a general thing to be found in the field, and under those circumstances I might just as well look for a needle in a haystack, therefore I made my search quite short.

On our return I was pleased to find a gentleman whose acquaintance I had long desired to make, he being no less than the Hon. Ezra Meeker, who has a world-wide reputation as being Washington's hop king. On being told the object of my visit, he gave me a kind reception. One of his foremen was immediately called up by telephone and dispatched to procure and bring to the office the object of my mission. A kindly invitation to dine with Mr. Meeker having been accepted I was escorted into a fine residence, that for modern architecture and furnishing, compares favorably with many of our eastern mansions. After being introduced to the most estimable lady and other members of the household, I began to realize that I was the guest of a household who had a beautiful home and knew how to enjoy it themselves, and to make their guests feel that a proper share was extended to them.

After tea I was presented with a formation (diseased root) resembling as to shape a medium sized watermelon cut in two in the center. The outside was covered somewhat with a hard, gristly substance, the inside or hollow portion being composed of a softer substance. This curious specimen (weighing three and one half lbs.) was found in the hill, just under the ground with the hollow side down, with many brace and fiber roots shooting out, seemingly for the purpose of furnishing nourishment to this odd freak of nature. The main vine was attached to the top side and this specimen was apparently the source from which the main vine received its nourishment. Mr. Meeker having described the disease to me previous to my having seen it, I ventured what I attributed to be the cause. This being the case I was somewhat anxious to make my predictions correct. This part of the investigation I will submit to Mr. Meeker as to whether I was correct or not. Those desiring further information pertaining to this part of my subject, I have the honor of referring to the hop king of Washington. Taking some of the decayed substance, similar to puss, out of the hollow part and placing it under my glass, I found two species of insects, one a tiny, little glossy, white, transparent magot. The other specimen was a little, somewhat transparent, louse, being not unlike, in many respects, some species of the aphis family, but being more closely related to the *Phyloxera* that has done so much damage in France. I am of the opinion that it might be named the "*Hop Phyloxera*," and not miss its calling, as I am satisfied that there was at least 20,000 of these little insects to be found in this one specimen, the louse being the most numerous.

This disease is not a fungus. The knots caused by the woolly aphis might as well be called fungus growth, from the fact that it is the aphis that forms a sore on the tree by forming colonies and concentrating their force in one spot, keeping up one (or many) continual sapping in the one place, and the tree putting forth one continual effort to heal the wound inflicted by its enemy, in order to do so produces a growth which forms a knot.

Remove the cause and if the tree is in good growing condition it will soon have healed over the wound, forming a sound, solid knot (not fungus). The disease in the hop is practically the same. If the tree is too far gone, dig it up and burn it. Don't pile it in the fence corner. Examine the hop roots and where there is to be found warts or lumps as big as a goose egg, dig them up and burn them. Where they are to be found smaller and less diseased, use the same treatment as prescribed for woolly aphis and you will soon conquer this terrible disease.

During my visit to the city of hops, I had the pleasure of an interview with Mr. Chas. Ross and his brother Mr. Ross, staying with the latter over night, receiving the usual kindness shown me which makes Washington farmers noted for their hospitality. These gentlemen are extensive hop growers and prosperous farmers, Mr. Chas. Ross being a member of the State Board of Horticulture, and from my interview with him I don't hesitate to say, he is the right man in the right place.

DESTRUCTION OF THE FRUIT CROP.

Ten years ago, Oregon was noted for its prolific apple crop, and the beautiful red and lucious fruit of that state was celebrated all over the Pacific Coast, from Alaska to the Gulf of California, and from the Pacific ocean to the Rocky mountains. This was before the codlin moth and the aphis appeared in the orchards. A worm-eaten apple was then the exception, but now it is the rule. The apple crop had never been a failure and the trees were yearly burdened with their weight of enticing fruit. Ten to fifteen bushels to the full-bearing tree was not extraordinary, and the farmer and horticulturist always found a ready market at good prices for the product of the orchard; sure fruit crop brought abundant reward. Things have changed since the advent of the destructive insects; the apple trees are no longer bowed down with the precious load; sound apples are a rarity; the big red apples of Oregon are a myth. The orchards that yielded profit are now profitless, and the farmers question whether to destroy the trees or leave them stand, monuments of past glory; victims of myriads of pestiferous insects.

The question of how to clean the orchards of Oregon, Washington and the whole country, now confronts the orchardist. The pests are everywhere, and they are industriously working while the fruit raiser is negligent. There is scarcely a fruit tree in the country that is not the breeding ground of these pests, and the fate of the Oregon apples will be the fate of the fruit of every section of the Pacific coast states.

The pests are here, and they are here to stay, unless united and intelligent effort is made to get rid of them. They are multiplying yearly by the million, and their multiplication means the destruction of the fruit interests of the whole country.

It may illustrate, to a certain extent, how widespread this fruit plague is if I quote at this point several articles bearing upon this subject, published in newspapers in various states. They are taken almost at random but will probably cover the point.

INSECT PESTS IN SEATTLE.

"Seattle, Jan. 10, 1893.

To the Editor of the Post-Intelligencer: I have of late inspected Seattle from center to circumference. I have now before me 100 twigs taken from 100 yards of this city, commencing at a point close to Grace M. E. church, near Lake Washington, thence to Jackson street, branching off on Bush, Sutter, Taylor and Wilfred streets, returning to Jackson street and following it to 9th, thence on 9th to James; thence on James to 6th, 5th and 4th, missing no yard in my line of investigation having any fruit, shade or ornamental trees worthy of note. On examination what do I find. Here on the apple twig I find 50 scales, known to me as the "cottony cushing scale." They seem to have but little choice as to the tree or shrub they infest. I have just found them in incalculable numbers on apple, pear, plum and cherry trees and currant bushes; also on thorn, elm, poplar, willow and mountain ash trees. The soft maple, however, is entirely exempt. This scale may be easily mistaken for the woolly maple bark louse, as described in the first biennial report of the Washington State Board of Horticulture, pages 87 and 88. Here you find their eggs in deposits of from 700 to 1000, small, white and spherical. The cottony cushing scale deposits from 200 to 500, rarely 700. The young (larvae) is dark red in color. The parent spins numerous ropes or balls of a white, cottony substance, the young scales taking up their temporary abode in this cottony mass, seemingly in order to receive heat and strength in the sunlight for a short time, after which, climbing up their silken web, they reach the limb, soon scattering broadcast over the tree, inserting the beaks into the tender twigs and leaves, poisoning and sapping the life of the tree. Three years ago I found the scale in but two yards of this city. Today I find them scattered broadcast. I am satisfied that there are millions now where there were thousands three and a half years ago. For a more concise description of this insect, consult our most eminent authorities, such as Prof. C. V. Riley, U. S. Entomologist, Comstock and others.

"Now holding another twig under my glass, what do I find. A living, crawling mass of little insects of a dark russet brown color, covered with a down of a cottony appearance. If there is any one curse greater than another in the way of fruit pests this is it. It is the woolly aphis. This insect confines its work of destruction to the apple tree. I have found them in countless millions on the wild crab tree of the forest. They infest the trunk, limbs and branches, forming knots all over the tree from the size of a pea to that of a goose egg. They are also subterranean and work at the roots of the trees, leaving them in the same condition as they leave the tops, thus in a short time completely ruining the tree. Three years ago I found them in a few yards in this city. Now I find them in many of our best yards, there being little, if any, effort put forth to get rid of them. I am satisfied that we have in this city 1000 for one we had three years ago.

"I now come to the oyster shell scale or bark louse, which you will find described in any of the bulletins issued by the State Board of Horticulture. I hold a twig in my hand which is eight inches in length, averaging half an inch in diameter. I estimate this twig to contain at least 1000 perfect scales. In turning one of these scales bottom side up it seems a hollow, empty shell of a dry, gluey appearance, but on further examination I find that this shell contains about 30 pretty white eggs. These are the eggs of the oyster-shell scale, which is scattered over our city. I leave an estimate to be made of the increase of 1894 over 1893 to some of the readers of this article, who may be better posted in figures than I am.

"I now hold in my hand an apple twig 12 inches in length. It has the appearance of being covered with a black, smutty substance. I have placed this twig under my glass, and the first thing that comes to my notice is a green louse. It is the honey dew aphis. It is midwinter, and still this pretty little green louse lives, moves and has its being on the fruit trees of our beautiful city. On further examination of this twig, I find that the black cast above described, is caused by thousands of little oblong, black, shining eggs. These are the eggs of the honey dew aphis. This is the cause, to a great extent, of the black cast that is given to our apple trees. These insects are not only bringing but have brought ruin to our apple orchards.

"I now hold in my hand a small twig of a prune tree, and to my old dim eyes it presents a reddish cast. On placing the twig under a glass, I find the eggs of the red spider, and if there is one little red egg there are 10,000 on this little prune twig. If this twig, four inches in length, contains 10,000 eggs, how many eggs are on the large sized prune tree that this twig was taken from. Then consult any of our prominent authorities and find what increase you may look for in the insect crop of 1894.

"I have now quit writing and gone to whittling. I have selected a fine, thrifty currant limb of last year's growth. The limb is 18 inches in length and averages half an inch in diameter. I have split the limb through the center. On doing so I find there is no pith in it, and on further investigation I find that what appears to have been the pith has taken the form of manure. I have split another twig; here I find the pith only gone in part. On a still further investigation I find the invader that is completely ruining the great majority of the currant shrubs of this city, and perhaps of the state. I have three very fine specimens crawling over my paper as I write. I say they are perfectly beautiful; my wife has just looked at them and she says they are perfectly disgusting, so this is where we differ. This is a white grub-like worm, a good half inch in length, not full grown, with a reddish or bronze colored head. This is the imported currant worm or borer. It does not subsist on the foliage and can well be called imported, from the fact that a young bush may look clean, healthy and thrifty, while at the same time from three to five young larvae are exploring the pith of each limb, and can easily be shipped to the far corners of the globe, unnoticed. There is another currant worm that is common in the east and very destructive, which is putting in an appearance in this state. This belongs to the saw-fly family, and is described as follows: *Nematus ventricosus*; family, *tenthredmidae*; sub-order, *hymenoptfera*. The yellow female saw-fly is about the size of a house fly, with a black head. She meets the smaller male, which has more black, and commences laying her whitish colored eggs along the veins underneath the leaf, about the first of May. These hatch in three or four days into green twenty-legged worms, dotted with black, until the last month, when they are entirely green. They commence immediately to feed on the leaves. These larvae eat voraciously and soon become full grown, being then three quarters of an inch long, when they either go into the ground, under the leaves, or remain attached to the bushes and spin a cocoon of brownish silk. The fly appears late in June or early in July and lays its eggs for a second brood, which comes forth before the end of the summer. These deposit their eggs; the caterpillars again feed on the leaves, mature and enter the ground, where they remain as panpau until the following spring, when the flies come forth to repeat the round of mischief. This insect may be called the imported currant worm, but if it is, I am not aware of the fact.

"I have neither time nor space to describe the ravages in our state of the tent caterpillar, peach, plum, apple and other borers. Neither have I space to describe the ravages of the codlin moth and other insects of a similar nature which are keeping pace with the other insects I have mentioned in this article. Nevertheless I feel as though I must mention one more insect, and that is the little rose-leaf hopper that is playing havoc with the beautiful rose bushes of our city. It is very small and cannot be seen by the naked eye. It is a little sap-sucker, and subsists on the sap it takes from the tender growth and leaves of the rose bush, giving the rose a white-spotted appearance. I have been asked by many ladies, "what is the matter with my rose bushes?" It is the little hopper, assisted somewhat by the rose aphis. If there were any of these hoppers here three years ago I failed to notice them.

"I presume that many statements that I have herein made will be questioned as to their being the whole truth and nothing but the truth. I would suggest that Gov. McGraw select a committee, composed of himself, chairman, Prof. Johnson, Entomologist of the State University, and all city editors. Then let that committee take a walk with me through a few of the yards of this city, and if I fail to prove the truth of the foregoing statements as a whole, I will admit to the public that I was in error, and I will make due apology to them. I am going to visit some of the hopyards in the near future, after which the readers of this article may hear from me again.

W. H. Brown."

FRUIT TREE PESTS IN UTAH.

Much has been said regarding insects that are devastating the fruit industry, not only of Utah, but all over the United States at the present time; and for this reason I wish to have a hearing through the columns of your valuable paper. I find that many of the old time citizens claim that a few years ago Utah had first class apples and peachs, not a worm to be found in an apple, and in 10 bushels of peaches and plums not a defective one was to be found. Now they say our fruit is no good. Why is this the case and where did these insects come from? I answer this question by stating that but few if any of these insects that are and have been destroying not only the world famed fruit of Utah, but the trees and shrubs as well, are natives of this territory. Then the question may be asked, as well as my statement criticised, where did they come from and how did they get here? Explain yourself. I answer this question by asking another: Where did our best citizens who are of foreign birth come from? The answer to this comes to me from the lips of every great and good American born citizen: From every civilized nation under the canopy of heaven (and some nations that are not civilized). I, without any hesitancy, concede the answer as given to my question, correct. But still another question, permit me to ask: Was there any distinction made between the great and good citizens of foreign birth and the low and depraved? Did not the same ship that carried many of the great minds of this nation, carry the murderer, the thief, and the scape-goats of all nations, and by so doing have we not become a dumping ground and a cess-pool for all nations? So it is with the fruit, shade and ornamental trees that have been shipped into our country. Go with me to some of our best parks in this nation and I will show you trees, shrubs and plants, that represent every clime which civilization has reached; and on most of these trees, shrubs and plants, I will show you an insect that represents every clime in the civilized world. There was no distinction made between the tree, plant or shrub that was free from this multifarious and pestiferous family, and the tree, shrub or plant that was free from those insects. I do not wish to be understood to say that all the mean people come from other countries, or that all injurious insects come from other nations; we have our share of both. My claim is that many of the worst insects are being palmed off on us, for instance, the woolly aphis, the American blight. This insect is one of the very worst insects that the apple tree is subjected to and was known in Europe a hundred years before America was discovered. This insect is to be found scattered broadcast over three-fourths of the apple orchards of the United States. The San Jose, or pernicious scale, was first found at San Jose, Cal., hence it derives its name from the fact that it was first discovered there. There is no doubt that this insect came from South America. The phylloxera has laid waste many of the vineyards of France for years and now this disease, the worst of all diseases, is in our midst. The gypsy moth is also an insect of foreign birth. This escaped from the cage of one who, I presume, thought he was going to confound the wisdom of the wise in his investigation of insect life. Now it has become such a plague in some of the eastern states that the inhabitants of whole counties turn out in picnic parties and a war of extermination waged. I have neither time nor space to make mention of the imported currant worm and other insects of a similar nature that are too numerous to mention. The question that would be most interesting to the reader of this article, is what kind of insects are to be found in Utah. I have this to say: That I have spent over three months investigating this question in four counties in this territory and that after a more prolonged investigation I will attempt at least to inform my readers on this subject. W. H. BROWN,

Practical Entomologist.

—*Deseret News*. May 6th, 1894, Salt Lake, Utah.

WHY FRUIT TREES DIE.

"Seattle, July 26, 1894.

"To the Editor: The *Post-Intelligencer* of Wednesday, the 25th inst, contained the following:

"Tacoma, July 24.—[Special.]—Owing to the large number of requests from Washington fruit growers and the State Board of Horticulture, the United States government, department of pathology, has arranged to send Newton B. Pierce to this state to investigate the cause of the destruction of the great number of trees. Most of the diseased trees are between two and three years old."

"As a man who has had considerable experience in this line, I take upon myself the responsibility to give your readers my opinion, so far as one reason is concerned. I take it for granted that all the readers of your journal who are horticulturists, and those who are not, are aware of the fact that there is vegetable and animal life. Take animal life, and you will find the whole make-up of the general composition is a very delicate piece of handiwork by the Creator. When disease sets in this wonderful piece of machinery requires a skillful physician to make the necessary repairs. So it is with the vegetable kingdom. Take a young tree; it is in its infancy; it has the same relationship to the parent tree in many respects that the child has to the parents. The stock is tender, the leaves are tender, while in the nursery row. For a mother to say: "I am going to wean my baby," often means death to her offspring, and more especially if she gives it too strong food. A physician may give twenty grains of quinine to the mother and she may not die; give it to the child and in all probability it means death. So it is in regard to young trees; to take the young tree from the nursery row is to dig it up by the roots. To plant it in new ground means new food. Perhaps the ground is too rich, perhaps too poor, perhaps too dry, perhaps too wet, perhaps killed by too much care and perhaps no care at all.

"Perhaps the poor tree has been a little ailing, and a physician was called, who felt its pulse, looked at its tongue, sounded its lungs and pronounced the disease consumption—prescribed for an old tree and not a young one. The dose he gave it was too strong and he killed the patient. Let me ask, what is more tender than the young leaves of a tree?

"The leaves are the lungs; these are one mass of pores. Place them under a powerful glass when it is 120 degrees in the shade, when it is very dry, and you will find these little valves open and shut; this means gasping for breath.

"I have before me a prescription prescribed by a physician of trees for those lungs. Let us see what it is: 'Take one pound of sulphur, one pound of concentrated lye and two pounds of whale oil soap, add to this twenty-five gallons of water. Apply this to the lungs (leaves).' A pretty strong tonic. The physician who prescribed this prescription evidently believes in either 'kill or cure,' as it has about one-fourth pound of the combined strength to a gallon of water.

"But let me ask, what is more tender than the fibrous roots of a young tender tree? These tender roots feel their way down into the ground, deeper and deeper, in search of nourishment, feeling their way into the crevices of rocks, Nature's aim being to sip up from Mother earth the rich juices that go to make up the woody substance of the tender rose shrub, or the 1000 growths that may be counted in the animal growths that go to make up the giant of the forest. Let me ask again what is more tender than those little fibers? Expose them to the hot sun a few minutes and they become as dry as powder. And yet those tender rootlets are dug up by the nurseryman and unavoidably exposed to the wind, weather and sun. The nurseryman perhaps knows that there is a law requiring him to supply his customers with disinfected nursery stock, and he must disinfect his stock before shipping to them. Fearing that there might possibly be some insects of a pestiferous nature, he concludes to use a disinfectant. Reading over the many doctor books in his possession, he comes to the following prescription, 'Take two gallons of water, put into this one pound of sulphur, add to this one pound of concentrated lye, also fish oil one half gallon, kerosene oil one-half gallon. After properly made add to this eight gallons of water.'

"Here you have about nine gallons of water when made to nine pounds of the compound medicine, making about one pound to each gallon of the emulsion. The trees are dipped into this emulsion, let stand long enough to kill all insects, which it will almost always do, as well as searing all the rootlets, as well as the bark on the tender limbs of the tree. Perhaps this work was not done in the nursery, but by the farmer before planting. Then a hurrah and cry goes up, 'Our young trees are dying.'

"Use less strong medicine on the young tender leaves, limbs and rootlets, and you will have less young trees die in Washington. W. H. BROWN."

NO MORE PESTS.

Prof. W. H. Brown, an expert horticulturist and entomologist of St. Paul, Minnesota, arrived in San Jose yesterday and located at the St. James Hotel. He is the inventor of "Prof. Brown's Insect Exterminator," which has proven a great boon to orchardists wherever used. He was here last June and several leading orchardists were given an exhibition of the wonderful efficacy of his destroyer of fruit pests. Prof. Brown's insect exterminator has met with all possible success. It has been used extensively from St. Paul to Portland, Oregon, and not a single failure to kill all insects on the trees sprayed has occurred. In St. Paul Prof. Brown was called upon to investigate the cause of the decay of the beautiful trees in public parks. He found half a dozen varieties of insect pests at work on them. Treatment with the exterminator killed all the pests and the trees again thrived. For this work he received columns of praise in the papers and thanks of the people. His remedy was used on fruit trees with like gratifying result. There was not an insect known to horticulturists that did not succumb to its deadly effect, while the leaves and blossoms of the trees sprayed were entirely uninjured. When Mr. Brown started west with his remarkable preparations he carried with him letters of unqualified indorsement from nearly all of the leading men of St. Paul and many other sections of the state. Among them are Mayor Smith, Judges Chandler and Gilfilin, Gen. J. H. Bishop, Archbishop Ireland, Ex-Governor Ramsey and many others who have seen the benefits of the exterminator. The same success has attended the efforts of Prof. Brown in all the other states. When trees are sprayed with his exterminator not a pest remains. He has testimonials from the leading orchardists of Oregon. E. W. Allen, of Portland, Secretary and Assistant Inspector of the State Board of Horticulture, enumerates a number of orchards visited by him which were so badly infested with San Jose scale, woolly and green aphis that he thought it was impossible to reclaim them. He recites that the trees were sprayed by Prof. Brown, all of the insects killed and the trees became as healthy as the best. Mr. Allen concludes thus: "I regard the wash used by you as very effective in the destruction of all insect pests and most heartily recommend its use by all who have trees or shrubs infested with insects injurious to them. I desire to thank you and those associated with you for the very effective and thorough work done in our orchards and yards in ridding them of the noxious insects that have infested them."

Dr. J. R. Cardwell, President of the Oregon State Board of Horticulture, indorses the statement of the secretary. He has also letters in the strongest words of praise of his exterminator, from the individuals whose trees and shrubs were so successfully treated. When here last June, Professor Brown visited the orchard of Col. Philo Hersey, President of the West Side Fruit-grower's Association, and the result is given in the following words, by Col. Hersey himself: "I hereby certify that Prof. W. H. Brown sprayed a prune tree that was badly infested with brown apricot scale, hatched and on the leaves. His spray, whatever it might be, began to show its effects as soon as dry. After three days I have this day examined many leaves and do not find a living scale. One twig on another tree, all of which was afflicted with the live scale on the leaf, was sprayed and the same results found on the leaves of the twig. The woolly and rose aphis immediately yielded to his treatment." A. Block, of Santa Clara also testified to the fact that trees of his infested with plum aphis and woolly aphis were successfully treated. From here Prof. Brown went to Watsonville and operated extensively in the Pajaro valley and elsewhere in Santa Cruz, the same remarkable success attending his efforts. James Waters, owner of the Pajaro Valley Nursery, wrote a strong testimonial, as did also W. H. Bowman, owner of the Corralitos nursery, who was so well pleased that he bought the right for Santa Cruz county. Geo. W. Sill, of Watsonville, who is well-known here, writes: "I do not hesitate to say that it is the most wonderful remedy ever applied to a tree or shrub, having seen it destroy woolly aphis, green aphis, plum aphis, codlin moth, black and brown scale, and hop lice in trees that had been washed with exterminators such as salt, sulphur and lime, rosin wash, I. X. L. and other exterminators such as have been used and recommended throughout our state and had failed to exterminate, his remedy killing instantly and leaving the tree and foliage in a good, clean and healthy condition. The trials have shown that there is not an insect known here that cannot be destroyed by one spraying with the exterminator." With this remedy at hand there is no excuse for pests of any kind whatever in the orchards, parks or gardens of the country and there is no doubt that its advent here will prove one of the greatest boons to orchardists.—*San Jose* (Cal.) *Mercury*, July 23, 1892.

TREES HAVE "THE GRIP."

"'We will soon have to commence doctoring the trees in the parks,' said W. A. Van Slyke, president of the board of park commissioners to a *Globe* reporter yesterday. 'You doubtless have discovered,' he continued, 'that the trees all over the city are ailing.'

"The reporter had done a good deal of lounging in the shade during the past few months, and, of course, had his sympathy aroused by the 'rocky' appearance of the horticultural specimens.

"'Trees are liable to derangements of their vital functions,' said the parkist, 'just as men are. Just now the trees all over the city are troubled with the grippe—if you choose to say so—and it doesn't require a microscope to show the worms that are destroying them. The trouble is due to prevailing ignorance rather than carelessness. People have their trees trimmed and cared for by men who don't know the first rudiments of tree culture, and the result is the trees die. We had some trouble with the trees in Smith park—though it did not cost the city anything extra. The contractor who furnished the trees had to replace the dead ones at his own expense. In some cases the trees were not planted properly (the roots having insufficient moisture and nutriment), and in other cases the trees were beset by worms. I took Prof. W. H. Brown, a scientific tree culturist, up to Smith park, and he extracted from one tree nearly a half-pint of the most villainous looking worms, conspicuous among them being the deadly "central wood borer." We revived one tree by placing among its roots an irrigating and fertilizing apparatus similar to those in the state capital grounds. The trees in Rice park will have to be treated in the same way, as they stand in "made ground," the fertility of which has become exhausted. Last August I noticed that one of the noble shade trees in Rice park was dying. I hastened to procure the best medical aid by summoning Prof. Brown. He called attention to the fact that the leaves, which he called the lungs of the tree, were all falling off. The tree would have to die for want of breath if something were not done at once. A myriad of small parasites were at work on the tender underside of the leaves. A solution was thrown over the trees with a hose and sprinkler, the parasites were killed, and the tree revived, and is alive today. The trees in the Summit avenue boulevard have got to be looked after, and, in fact, the trees all over the city need immediate and careful attention.'

"A HORTICULTURIST TALKS.

"Prof. W. H. Brown, horticulturist and entomologist, was next seen, and he talked quite interestingly as follows:

" 'The present invasion of the tree-destroying worms is not the first that has afflicted us. The first visitation was about fifteen years ago. Again the pest came seven years ago, again two years later, and again last summer. I estimate that the damage done to trees by worms alone in St. Paul and Minneapolis during the past year will amount to $100,000. At the request of Col. Van Slyke, Ald. Cullen, Ald. Melady and others, I have just made a thorough examination of the trees in Central Park, and out of 193 trees find 83 seriously affected, and others lightly by worms. I do not think this is due to negligence, but to ignorance on the part of the man who has the care of the trees. The trouble might have easily been averted. The trees are chiefly affected on the south side, and many of them are past saving.

" 'I have found thirteen different kinds of worms, belonging to a family of 360 varieties. The way in which these worms get into the trees is chiefly through the cracking of the bark by the alternate thawing and freezing at this season. The sun warms the south side of the tree by day and starts the sap. The frost freezes it at night. The sap—especially of maples, box elders and other sugar-bearing trees—flows into the opening and forms a jelly in which the beetles love to deposit their eggs. The eggs hatch and the grubs devour the sweet stuff, and then explore the tree looking for more. The same results may be produced by having the tree trimmed by an ignorant person, who will cut off a branch and leave the wound uncovered. A large number of fine trees in this city have thus been ruined.'

"BLIGHT IN FRUIT TREES.

"When questioned about blight among fruit trees, Prof. Brown said:

" 'I'll answer that question by stating that there has been a very great deal of trouble experienced from blight to apple trees. When I sold my farm at Fulda, Minn., to Archbishop Ireland, there were seventy-five apple-bearing trees upon the place, and there was not a single tree among them that had a blighted limb. I now reside at No. 749 Gorman avenue, St. Paul, where you may see in flourishing condition ten apple trees that I have owned for three years. Among them are the Duchess, Transcendent and Siberian types. They bear apples every year, and they have never been affected by blight or worms since I became the owner of them. I would be happy to have them inspected by all interested persons.

" 'There is another influence at work destroying the shade trees of these two cities, and especially have I noticed this in St. Paul where there never has been any excess of fertile earth. The influence of which I speak is lack of food and drink. That was the chief trouble with the trees in the capitol grounds, before the tanks were placed at their roots. So great is the reverence felt for trees, you have noticed some grand old trunks towering up through the stone sidewalks in certain localities? Those monarchs must all die unless something is done for them. The water cannot reach their roots, and there is no way to get nutriment with the limestone underneath, the curbstone on the side and the Portland stone up above the roots. The building of sewers and the paving of streets has a tendency to drain off the moisture necessary to the health of a shade tree, and the custom of continually mowing and raking the lawns shuts off the supply of Nature's ordinary fertilizers, i. e., decayed grass and leaves. Hence you see trees and sward so often looking sickly. Both trees and terraces should be watered and fertilized by underground tanks and perforated pipes. When the water is sprinkled upon the surface, the sun drinks it up faster than the earth; especially is this true of watering trees. A bucket of water placed in a tank among the roots of a tree will do more good than several barrelsful poured upon the surface of the ground.' "—*St. Paul Globe*, April 13, 1890.

DEATH TO TREE PESTS.

Prof. W. H. Brown, of St. Paul, professional shrub and tree forester, entomologist, and patentee of Brown's Irrigator and Fertilizer and Insect Exterminator, who has been operating in this part of the country for the past eight months, yesterday gave a practical illustration of his methods upon the fruit trees in the yard of ex-mayor Henry Yesler. It is a well-known fact that two of the greatest industries of this country, hop raising and fruit growing, are being threatened with destruction by little insects which cluster in thousands and tens of thousands upon the branches and leaves. Cherry and apple trees in particular are effected by these insect pests, and prunes and hops are falling in for their share. If the insects are not promptly destroyed they will work great injury to the trees and eventually kill them. Yesterday Prof. Brown demonstrated very clearly that he was a physician of trees, one who has made it a life study and treated infested trees in a manner that was logical and thorough. He exhibited to the reporter a number of twigs cut from Mr. Yesler's trees before he had used his exterminating wash. One cherry twig about 12 inches in length and as big as a man's little finger, was completely covered with little brown specks, oblong in form. These the professor called oyster shell scale, and when he lifted one up, about 6 or 8 little white specks were visible and these, the Professor said, were eggs. When hatched they become sap-sucking insects and would suck the very life blood out of the tree. On the twig mentioned, the professor said there was fully 10,000 insects, only waiting to develop before commencing their disastrous explorations of the tree. A twig and blossom from a prune tree was next exhibited, and, with the aid of a microscope thousands of little insects could be seen in the smallest conceivable space. These the professor pronounced to be hop aphis, which do such an incalculable amount of damage to trees and hops. They will sap the vines and tender branches, the blossoms and leaves of fruit trees, and play havoc generally with hops. Shrubs or any plants cannot hope to escape these insects, and the entire business of horticulture, fruit and hop raising, is threatened by them. The trees which the professor had operated on by spraying were next examined, and in every case the tree was wholly free from insects of any nature. The spray had done its work well, for every one of the little pests that the spray had come in contact with had taken a noiseless flight to insect heaven. One thing that attracted the reporter's notice was the fact that the delicate white blossoms of the apple trees, although they had become thoroughly saturated with the exterminating fluid, had not been injured in any wise, but looked brighter and more vigorous than before. Prof. Brown's patent irrigator and fertilizer is a uniquely constructed apparatus and is put together in such a logical manner that the theory is perfect in all its details. He feeds and doctors the tree from its roots, and, first finding out what a tree wants, supplies it. In every case success of a flattering nature has attended his efforts.

Mr. Yesler, in speaking of the work of the professor, said: "Satisfied? Well, that is a poor expression. I have never been so well pleased in all my life, and will be pleased to be able to recommend Prof. Brown to any one who has infested trees. He is one of the most thorough workmen I have ever seen, and does not make one single promise he does not fulfill. I have learned more about insects to-day than I ever knew before, and that knowledge is worth a great deal to me. Had not the professor taken hold of my fruit trees I am inclined to think they would have all died. He stands in the light of a public benefactor, for while he is following the business as a profession he is ridding the country of pests which number hundreds in variety and which have been steadily on the increase. With the professor's exterminating fluid on hand, hop raisers and fruit growers need not fear that their crops are going to be a discouraging failure."
—*Seattle Post-Intelligencer.*

WORKS LIKE A CHARM.

Prof. W. H. Brown used his insect and aphis exterminator with deadly effect to all insect life in the orchard of John F. Kincaid, during the early part of this week. On many of the trees the branches were literally black with eggs before treatment, but not three per cent. of the insects or eggs remain. Mr. Kincaid is highly pleased with Prof. Brown's work and takes pleasure in urging all fruit growers who wish to save their trees and have fully developed fruit, to arrange to have them treated by Prof. Brown. W. C. Kincaid was present when the work was being done, and he unhesitatingly pronounces it a complete insect exterminator..—*Sumner Herald*, April 17, 1891.

A PEST EXTERMINATOR IN CALIFORNIA.

We published yesterday an interview with Prof. W. H. Brown, an expert horticulturist and entomologist of St. Paul, Minnesota, in regard to an insect exterminator of which he is the inventor. The subject is one of great importance to all fruit growers. Even in this country where the intelligently directed zeal of our orchardists and orchard inspector, have kept the trees almost absolutely free from all kinds of pests, the new exterminator will be found worthy of careful consideration. A man with a well filled tank may have an abundant supply of water to put out a fire, and yet if he deals in inflammable goods he does not neglect to pay attention to every appliance, for extinguishing fires, that science can invent. So it is with our fruit growers, pests are comparatively unknown in this valley, but none the less any mode of treatment that renders it easier to destroy them in case they should occur, is of interest to us. Prof. Brown speaks with authority on the subject, and his remedy comes well recommended, but it should have a full and thorough test in this country, in order to see if the effect here will be as good as it was elsewhere. The test, moreover, should be made at this time while the fruit and leaves are on the trees, as it is only in this way that it can be determined whether in exterminating the pests it may not also injure the trees or the fruit. Most remedies for the pests are applied in the winter time when the trees are bare, and as a consequence, it is impossible to note what effect they have upon the tree itself and upon the fruit that is to come. Such a test, of course, is not so conclusive as one made at this season, and for that reason our orchardists should subject Prof. Brown's exterminator to a trial right away. The Professor was in this county some time ago, and his exterminator was at that time tried by Col. Hersey and by A. Block, both of whom report favorable results and unite in recommending it. This, of course, is a strong point in its favor, but a wider trial should be given it. Our leading fruit men should take up the question and test it thoroughly. We may not need anything of the sort very badly at this time, but if there is a remedy for pests that is readily applied and will not injure fruit or trees it will be well for our fruit growers to know it, for there may come a time when they will need it badly.—*San Jose (Cal.) Daily Mercury*, July 24, 1892.

DISCOURSE ON INJURIOUS INSECTS.

On Monday afternoon, March 12, Prof. Brown, of Seattle, Wash., delivered a lecture in the East Bountiful Tabernacle on the subject of insects injurious to fruit culture, etc. The professor spoke on the different kinds of insects that destroy our fruit trees and shrubbery. He said that there is a class of insects that live on the branches, stems, and roots of trees while there are other classes that live on the leaves of the trees. The speaker explained that the leaves of a tree are the lungs of the tree, and that each leaf contained a countless number of small openings or pores from which these insects suck the life blood of the tree. One cause of fruit and berries falling to the ground before they are ripe, the professor claimed, was the insects getting on the stems of the fruit and sucking the sap from the same. The speaker had gathered a number of twigs from the orchards in the neighborhood, which he showed to members of the audience under a microscope. It was found that they were fairly alive with these destructive little pests. He thought that it was on account of our neglectfulness that we had so many wormy apples. The professor said that these insects should be destroyed by using Insect Exterminator. He recommended that the rough bark on the apple trees be removed now and the tree sprayed, and that the tree be sprayed again just as the blossoms are falling off. If we would treat our trees after this manner the speaker thought we again could raise sound apples. Prof. Brown said that if California did not pay more attention to the subject of destroying insects than the people of Utah had done, that the fruit growing industry of that state would not be in as prosperous a condition as it is now. He said that we should export instead of import fruit; that our climate and soil were suitable to make fruit growing in Utah the leading industry.

The people in the various settlements in the county would do well to invite Prof. Brown to talk to them on the above mentioned subject.—*Davis County (Utah) Clipper*, March 12, 1894.

THE HOP PEST.

In a recent talk with Wm. H. Brown, a prominent horticulturist, he had the following to say of the hop aphis:

"Ever since the hop aphis put in an appearance in our state there has been a great deal of speculation as regards its being the hop aphis that has done so much damage to the hop crop in Europe, also at times destroying and laying waste the hop industry of New York and Wisconsin and other portions of the United States and having had no small experience with this pest in the east. Therefore on my arrival in this state three years ago, being informed that the hop aphis had put in its appearance in the hop yards of White river valley, I immediately commenced a thorough investigation.

"I found that a partial loss of the hop crop that year had caused some of the hopgrowers great alarm as to their true identity, some having written to prof. C. V. Riley, United States entomologist, on the subject. The professor, in reply, gave them a short sketch of the life, history and habits of this pest. In Mr. Riley's reply he stated that this aphis confined its winter deposit to the prune and plum. This statement I concluded to be a fact, so far as their deposit in the east is concerned, but so far as their deposit in the Sound country is concerned I differ, from the fact that on a prolonged investigation lasting over three months, I failed to find an aphis deposit on prune or plum. Had I found a deposit on this class of trees then there might have arisen a question in the minds of the many entomologists who may be able to classify the different species of this multifarious family.

"Therefore, when I was found to differ with men whose knowledge and experience stands second to none in the United States, and perhaps in the world, I soon began to realize that I was in the midst of a hornet's nest, some of the hopgrowers going so far as to ask me would I dare to presume to question Prof. Riley's decision on this question.

"My answer to this was: I am a citizen of the United States and fought for the liberties that I enjoyed, one of which was a right to a difference of opinion when thoroughly satisfied that I was in the right.

"I have just returned from a two week's visit in the orchards of Whatcom county, where I had the pleasure of meeting many old friends from Minnesota. I visited many of the prominent orchardists in the vicinity of Custer, one of whom is Judge Pratt, who is also the owner of a beautiful 15-acre fruit ranch, situated in the city that stands second to none for push and enterprise on this coast (the city of Seattle).

"In visiting Mr. C. H. Sotolienberg I found that this gentleman stands among the many who rank among the first in the great army of fruit growers (1500) who are destined to make Whatcom county one of the greatest fruit growing counties on the Pacific coast.

"I visited many orchards and one hop ranch in the vicinity of Blaine, Custer and Ferndale, and made a thorough examination for the hop aphis, but failed to find an aphis deposit on either prune or plum trees. I found the deposit of red spider, plum, curculio, oyster shell scale, black fungus, bark borers, central wood borers and the peach curl leaf.

"Stopping at Orilla I visited Mr. Nelson. I found that this gentleman had finished pruning the limbs, piled in bunches, which gave me a splendid opportunity to find an aphis deposit, but on careful examination I failed to find an aphis egg on prune or plum.

"I then visited Pat Hayes. I found that Mr. Hayes had about finished pruning a ten acre prune orchard. I found in this fine orchard two scrub plum trees that had been planted by an Indian. Those trees were infested with an aphis deposit, the rest of the orchard being free from this pest as far as I could see.

"I don't wish to be understood as saying that there is no such deposit on the prune or plum, I simply say that the deposit, if any, is not enough to justify the hop-growers in thinking that to clear his prunes or plums is all he need do to get rid of the hop louse. This theory in my opinion is all bosh. The question may be asked if there is so scarce a winter deposit on the prune and plum, how is it that both prune and plum are infested with aphis (larvae)?

"This question carries with it as much mystery as that of the hop aphis. My opinion is that the perfect fly makes her deposit on the foliage and not on the twig, the same as the hop aphis.

"Another question may be asked: Will this argument hold good east of the mountains on the Pacific slope? This is a question in my mind, from the fact that their winters are different from ours, they being like eastern winters, and from the fact that while at Boise City, Idaho, I examined a large young prune orchard that is infested with an aphis that is covered with a scanty covering of white silky down, so that when brought in contact with water the water rolls off like water from a duck's back. The under side of the leaf affected is covered with a very fine silken spider-like web. This is a genuine plum aphis, but it has just a little more downy covering, than I ever saw on a prune aphis before, and it is my opinion that this insect will confine its deposit to the prune and plum alone. Let me say to the readers of this article in conclusion, what I know about insects would make a small book and what I don't know would make a large one. Nevertheless, I am not done with this investigation as regards the hop aphis and insects injurious to the fruit industry.

"I will solve this question if it takes me all summer. I leave Monday at 9 p. m. for Salt Lake City to investigate some kind of blight. When satisfied what species of blight this is, the readers of this article will hear from me again."—*Seattle News*, Feb. 21st, 1894.

LIFE AND HABITS OF ANTS.

WRITTEN BY REQUEST.

Ants are generally found in colonies, very rarely in pairs. They are of three distinct sexes, namely—males, females, and neuters. The neuters, or soldiers, do all the work and also defend the nest from enemies. The males and females constitute but a small portion of the inhabitants of the hill, and are provided with bright glistening wings, whereas the workers have no wings. The workers are not so large as the males and the females are larger than the males. Some species of the neuters and females are provided with a sting, others that have no sting are armed with a little sack, situated in the abdomen, which is filled with a foul-smelling and poisonous fluid, which they squirt at the offender. This fluid has been known to kill small animals, and dogs have been known to rush from the place yelling. The habitation of the ant is a very curious and ingenious affair, many of them displaying great intelligence. The majority live in the ground and gradually rise to the surface, extending up as high as 15 or 20 feet in some countries, and others (the red and horse ant) construct their hills till they are about the size of a small hay-cock. The hill is usually originated by two or three queens (like the bee), who lay in the spring and continue all summer, after which the males and females leave the nest in great swarms, the male dying soon after, seeming to have completed his mission.

These little enemies of the garden are very active and might serve to teach many of us the value of utilizing every moment, many of which we often waste. Solomon says, "Look to the ant, thou sluggard, consider her ways and be wise." The winged ants are short lived, coming in autumn and dying when the cold weather commences, except a very few that are left to carry on their work the next season. I think this is one of the ways in which the Creator shows His wisdom in preventing them from overrunning the country and doing more damage than they do.

When the ants are at work they keep up a continual humming, but it is so faint that myriads of them do not exceed the hum of one wasp. They are very warlike among themselves, and two colonies will sometimes have a battle, when on examing the ground around it will appear like a miniature human battle-field, the killed and wounded lying around in great profusion, and the insects running around in all directions as though attending to the wounded soldiers. Sometimes the heads of the enemies will be severed from the body and fastened so tightly to the victor that the jaws cannot be gotten open and so they have to carry around with them the bloody evidences of the contest. Some of the heads have life long after they are separated from the body, and bite viciously at the enemy.

There is a great deal of kidnapping practised among the ants, the red ant being especially noted for this. It will often carry away the pupa of other species, tend them as carefully as their own until full grown, when they are forced to labor. Some of the females that escape death from their enemies or by the elements in the fall start new colonies, while others are taken possession of by the neuters of the hill, near which they happen to be, and some think they go in search of them. When the neuters capture the female they rob them of their wings and they are forced to the habitation where they are fed and treated, like the queen bee, with apparent respect. There are also some ant hills that unlike the bees, contain numerous females who are treated thus and also carry on the important work of laying eggs. They are always deprived of their wings, sometimes by the neuters and not rarely by the female herself who finds them useless after she has produced her eggs. They also collect great numbers of the honey dew aphis and tend them for the sake of the honey which the aphis produces, and will even go so far as to protect it from a parasitic fly which attacks it, and in turn the aphis seems willing to yield the product of its labors to its captors. The ants are very fond of this honey and will climb trees in order to get at an aphis. They wait for drops to fall, and will, to make them fall, pat each side of the abdomen in turn quickly, then when the honey is ejected will go to another. This process has been compared to milking cows. The aphis is kept in quantities by ants, sufficient to supply the inhabitants of the hill, and are tended to with as much care as their own kind. This is so wonderful that it may be doubted by some, but nevertheless it has been observed and recorded by the most popular and careful scientists.

The egg of the ant is so small that to see it well one must be provided with a glass. The mother seems to take no thought about them, but drops them wherever she happens to be, and the neuters or workers, some of whom seem to be in continual attendance upon her, seize them as soon as dropped, moisten them with the tongue and pile them up in one part of the nest, all the time watching them and removing them from one part of the apartment to the other, probably keeping them at the right temperature or to keep them in just the dampness. It takes but a few days for the larvae to be produced, and then it is when the workers show their intelligence and tenderness in the care of the baby ants. The wonderful loving-kindness of the Creator is here shown by furnishing the workers with a fluid suitable for the young ants, which the neuters emit into the mouths of the larvae. They are also very careful to keep the brood clean by continually licking them. A great deal of labor is expended in taking them to the surface when the weather is suitable, and back again when it rains or grows cold. When an ant's nest is broken into, small while kernels resembling grains of barley are often seen being carried to places of safety, and are often thought to be the food which the ant lays up for winter use, but which is no less than pupa.

The pupa is enveloped in a silken cocoon, and unlike other insects requires help to extricate themselves. This help is usually given by the workers. The food of the ants (most always provided by the workers) is sometimes animal and sometimes vegetable. A very few specimens of ants store up grain and seeds, and when they do the germ is somehow destroyed or eaten by the ants so that it will not grow. Some ants carry chips, sticks and other things to build their nest with. Ants all seem to have a weakness for sugar and are guided by a fine sense of smell. This is why the housewife so often loses her temper when a swarm of these interesting little insects invade her pantry, then it is in vain she hears their cute habits discussed. At this time she would take more interest in learning how to rid herself of the pest.

Ants that live on animal food are sometimes useful in destroying other insects and devouring the dead bodies of small animals. Some have been known (in tropical countries) to strip the flesh off the bones of the larger animals and even human beings are sometimes in danger. A certain species in the island of Grenada, that made its appearance about 100 years ago, made its nest under the roots of plants and the sugar cane were rendered almost useless in consequence. They came from the hills in torrents, and plantations, paths, and miles and miles of roads were filled with them. Rats, mice and reptiles fell prey to their ravages. Streams of water were turned on them to no effect. Millions of fresh recruits were arriving every minute, and the drowned formed a dam sufficient for the newly arriving ants to climb over. Fire was then tried but with equal uselessness, for they rushed into the flames in such vast numbers as to put the fire out. Rewards were offered to any one who would suggest a successful exterminator, but to no purpose. They ruled the land until a hurricane, which occurred in 1780, tore up the sugar canes and exposed the ant hills to the deluge, thus ridding the island of this pest.

The ant lion is about the worst enemy with which the ant has to contend. It digs a hole in the sand and when the ant comes along, makes a disturbance which arouses its curiosity and going to the scene of commotion, the lion lashes the sand and so bewilders the ant that it falls into the pitfall and is soon grasped in the jaws of the lion.

The foregoing are only a very few thoughts, comparatively speaking, on this very interesting family of ants. Let me say in concluding that although this insect is very destructive, still it has, as have all of God's creation, a work to do and is in a certain degree useful. Ant baths are given for gout and paralysis by boiling crushed ants and immersing the affected limb in it.

NELLIE E. BROWN.

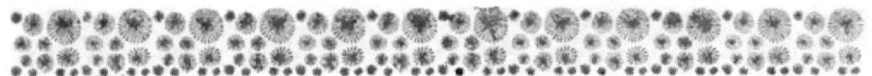

PART II.

The Insects That Destroy.

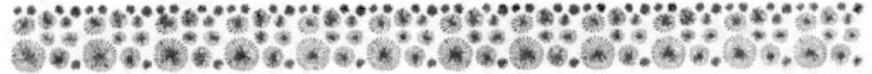

CODLIN MOTH.

In May or June these little gray moths make their appearance in the orchards, and as soon as the fruit forms, they deposit an egg on the blossom end of the fruit, and when the egg hatches, the larvæ enters the apple. The Bible informs us that Adam took the first bite of this somewhat seductive fruit, persuaded by Eve, but intelligent students of horticulture sometimes feel disposed to doubt the statement and assert that the codlin moth beat the record, and the worm got the first bite. This white worm, after eating its way through the fruit, leaves it, spins a cocoon and assumes a chrysalis state. It requires three weeks for the larvæ to mature, and fifteen days for the moth to issue from the chrysalis state. The apples are again stocked with eggs and the process of hatching repeated. The last generation remain in the cocoons until spring, when the same round is begun, the fruit rendered worthless and the horticulturist deprived of his fruit crop by the ravages of the pest. The codlin moth is conceded by all horticulturists to be one of the worst insects with which they have to contend. They are early and late workers, beginning with early spring and ending with the summer.

TREATMENT FOR CODLIN MOTH.

The arsenical compound should be used on codlin moth. This compound differs from the other compounds from the fact that there are four ounces of London purple added to 100 lbs. of the compound, making it somewhat poisonous, but not enough to make it dangerous to those who handle it. Neither is it dangerous to eat the fruit after it has been sprayed. The first spraying should be done when the blossoms begin to fall. In from seven to ten days repeat the same operation, and it may be necessary to repeat it once or twice more in from fourteen to twenty days, should the moth still be present. This will invariably insure a good crop of fruit. Dissolve one pound of the compound in from 8 to 10 gallons of water for repeated spraying on the codlin moth, as above described.

CANKER OR MEASURING WORM.

When full grown the measuring worm is about one inch long, of ash color, black and yellow. They belong to the loopers or measuring worm, both names being derived from their peculiar method of locomotion. They are called drop worms also, from their habit of swinging from limbs by a thread. They are the product of a moth of gray ash color which comes from the ground in the spring. These moths deposit eggs in the trunks of trees, often to the number of hundreds, and when the leaves are coming out the larvæ make their appearance and immediately begin to feed upon the foliage, completely stripping the tree. They attack fruit and ornamental trees as well, and after they have destroyed foliage, they burrow into the ground and in an earthen cocoon change to pupae, from which they emerge again in the spring in the shape of a moth.

REMEDY.

Spray for this insect as soon as the worms appear on the trees. Spray with arsenical compound, one pound to eight gallons of water. If this prescription is not strong enough to kill, make it stronger, if too strong make it weaker, put it on to kill whether it effects the foliage or not. Dig lime and guano into the ground around the base of the tree. Dissolve at the rate of four pounds of arsenical compound to 40 gallons of water, add four pounds of Babbit's lye, then saturate the ground around to a depth of eight inches. Spray trees in fall and winter as for scale. Do thorough work and you will get rid of them.

FALL WEB WORM.

In habit these insects are in some respects similar to the tent caterpillar, but are not so destructive in their habits. They feed upon all kinds of foliage. They come from the beautiful white moths, and are hatched in August. The worms are about an inch long when fully grown. They are striped with yellow and black and dotted with orange. They descend from the tree in October and disappear in the ground.

REMEDY.

No. 1 arsenical compound, as for codlin moth, and No. 2 as soon as the webs are to be seen. Cut and burn, and remember one thing, that to destroy a butterfly is to destroy hundreds of your worst enemies 98 times out of 100.

TENT CATERPILLAR.

In June and July the tent caterpillars make their appearance. The moths of this species are brown, the female being a little larger than the male, with two light bands running across the fore wings. They are attracted by lights and fly into houses during the warm summer evenings. The eggs are laid in clusters about twigs, covered with glue and impervious to water. The clusters are composed of about 400 eggs, which hatch just as the leaves of the apple and cherry trees are coming out. On these trees they weave their tents, and feed upon the foliage, generally destroying it. By the middle of June the worms attain their full size—about two inches in length, variously striped with yellow, blue and white. Their appetite is voracious, and after stripping the trees, they disperse, seeking hiding places where they form their cocoons undisturbed. They pupate almost immediately and in two weeks reappear as moths, with the same round of perpetuation and mischief.

REMEDY.

Use same remedy as given for the apple tree tent caterpillar.

WHITE SPOTTED TUSSOCK MOTH.

This insect is more familiar to the cities than the country, by reason of its being found on the shade trees and shrubbery of the cities; yet it is not confined to cities, nor is its ravages confined to shade trees alone. It is cream yellow in color, sometimes changing to white, with brownish spots and brush-like hairs and red head. There are also two long plumes rising from the head. Their cocoons are usually found in the rough bark of the trees.

REMEDY.

Use arsenical compound same as for codlin moth, during the fall and winter. The eggs may be seen in little white clusters. They may be destroyed in a great measure by cleaning off all rough bark and using medicine as directed for oyster shell scale.

CABBAGE MOTH.

The cabbage worm comes from the white rape butterfly, and mainly confine themselves to the destruction of cabbage. The butterflies come in two broods—the first in May, the second in August.

REMEDY.

When you see this pretty white moth flying over your cabbage you can soon begin to look for worms on your cabbage and the leaves riddled with holes. For this insect use at the rate of one pound of No. 14 compound to 8 gallons of soft water (warm) and apply with spray pump. Saturate well and you will soon have dead cabbage worms. Repeat as often as the worms put in their appearance. Keep them killed off this year and you will have none next year, that is, if your neighbor serves them likewise.

CABBAGE LOUSE, OR APHIS.

REMEDY.

Keep a careful watch in your cabbage patch, and as soon as you see the louse, commence spraying. Use No. 14 compound, one pound to 10 gallons of water. Melt in hot water, then add cold. Two or three sprayings will keep your cabbages clear from this pest.

APPLE TREE BORER.

There are two or more species of beetles that have done and are doing great damage to fruit trees all over the portions of the United States where I have traveled. The flat headed borer cuts its way between the bark and the wood, commencing on the south and southwest side of the tree. This species will ruin a tree in a very short time. The round-headed borer, is what is known as "the central wood borer", differing from the one first mentioned, from the fact that it has a round head. The eggs are laid in May, June and July, the flat head deposits her eggs about 18 inches above the base, while the round heads or central wood borers, deposit close to the base and work down the first year; the second year they change their course and work upward, boring their way into the wood as though for pastime, continuing their explorations until the third year, when they come out of their house of luxury; after which they soon become perfect beetles. They soon co-habit, deposit their eggs, and by so doing perfect their mission, being a great round of mischief.

REMEDY.

Scrape off all rough bark, mix one pound of arsenical compound to eight gallons of hot water, go over the stock and large limbs with a scrub brush. After this has been performed, take a pailful of the wash and add enough lime to make the tree look white, apply with a broom, spray or otherwise. Where the roots are affected apply same remedy to the roots as for peach borers. Apply remedy as soon as spring opens; again about the middle of June. If spraying for other insects saturate roots well at any time and the labor will not be in vain.

PEACH TREE BORER.

In July, August and as late as September, the peach tree borers make their appearance as a moth. They resemble wasps, being long and slender. They lay their eggs at the base of trees, and soon after larvæ will be found, and they will commence boring in the sapwood and back beneath the surface. The larvæ works till about the first of July, when pupæ encased in a cocoon composed of chip dust, earth and gum. The female is larger and darker than the male, with yellow band across the abdomen. The males are about an inch in length. They soon destroy the trees if not removed. Their presence in the trees is easily detected by the gum oozing out of the places they have been working.

REMEDY.

The presence of tree borers is made known by the gum oozing out around the knots and limbs of peach, plum and cherry trees.

For this tree pest use the same remedy as for woolly aphis, except the use of manure. A handful of coarse salt should be scattered at the base of the tree after the other work has been done. This work should be done in the fall or spring. Spray twice more during the spring or summer, using plenty of lime on the body and around the base of the tree. Care should be taken not to spray the foliage with lime.

ELM TREE BEETLE.

The elm tree beetles have become very destructive to trees recently, more especially in the Eastern cities. The trees afflicted become sickly and present a blighted appearance.

REMEDY.

Use No. 14 as for aphis.

ROSE BEETLE.

The rose beetle, or bug, is one of the worst pests encountered by the gardener. It attacks and devours leaves, buds and blossoms. Not confining itself to roses, it reaches out for peaches, grapes, cherries, vegetables, and what it cannot eat it blasts. The rose beetle is green and has a conical projection at the extremity of the body between the honey tubes, and the honey tubes are long. There are other varieties of the rose pest that are red, and still another—the rose hopper—that is white. The latter feeds exclusively on the leaves of the rose. They pupate, then again return in the hopper state after ten days. A third brood of the pests is produced in one season.

REMEDY.

Spray No. 14 at the rate of 10 gallons of water to one of the compound. Spray with arsenical compound, if not in bloom. Scattering hardwood ashes on bushes while the dew is on is a great preventative. Slacked lime will answer in place of ashes.

SQUASH BUGS.

This is an enemy of the garden familiar to all. It hibernates during the winter, but is on hand ready for business when the vines of the squash, pumpkins, melons and cucumbers are up. They hide at night in the ground and reappear in day time to feed upon the vines.

REMEDY.

Use No. 14. Use one pound to nine gallons of hot water; let cool and spray when necessary. Arsenical compound is better if you are not going to use the vegetation for some time.

WIRE WORMS.

The wire worms are destructive to corn, grass and potatoes. They are the larvae of the *elater*, or spring beetles, and usually feed on rotten wood.

REMEDY.

Use arsenical compound as for cut worms.

LEAF CRUMPLERS.

The presence of these pests on fruit trees is made known by the leaves presenting a brown and crumpled appearance. The leaves and limbs are drawn together and tied by the silken webs spun by the pests. The worm itself is housed within this nest, where it reproduces and feeds upon the foliage.

REMEDY.

Use same remedy as for codlin moth.

POTATO BUGS.

Potato bugs, while well known in Colorado and the East, are comparatively unknown on the Pacific Coast. It grows with the growth of the potato vine, appearing when the vine first comes out of the ground. The female produces about a thousand eggs on the underside of the leaves, which soon hatch, and the young larvae prove as destructive to the vines as the older members of the family. Fifteen days sees them fully developed.

REMEDY.

Use arsenical compound at the rate of 1 pound to 8 gallons of water; dissolve in 3 gallons of hot water. Stir with old broom till thoroughly mixed and dissolved, then add five gallons cold water. Spray the vines thoroughly.

THRIPS.

The thrip is a minute insect hardly visible to the naked eye, varying in color from whitish yellow to brown. They are very active. They confine themselves to plants that are in shady places and neglected.

REMEDY.

Same remedy as used for green aphis.

THE PLUM GOUGER.

Prof. C. P. Gillett, of the Iowa Agricultural Experiment Station, has made a complete study of this insect, of which the following report will be found of interest to plum growers:

The plum gouger is a western insect and is rarely if ever found farther east than Lake Michigan.

This insect in its mature state is a beetle, somewhat resembling, and frequently mistaken for the plum curculio. It varies from 7-32 to 8-32 of an inch in length. The wing covers are leaden gray in color and are more or less sprinkled with small black and brown spots. The head and throax are ochre-yellow in color and the snout and legs are reddish brown and are covered with short hairs. In fresh specimens there is a yellowish brown median line along the back on the borders of the wing covers of the same color as the throax. The rostrum or snout is slender, very slightly curved and about as long as the head and throax, or about 1 1-2 of an inch.

Spring appearance.—The beetle appears in the spring much earlier than the curculio. They feed on the buds and flowers. I have found by bringing the beetles into the laboratory and keeping them on fresh plum twigs that, since the flowers began to open, they feed entirely upon the ovaries of the buds and blossoms which they reach by puncturing the calyx. Six beetles in 24 hours punctured the calyces and ate the ovaries of 65 buds and blossoms.

As to the proportion of gougers in the fruit to the number of mature beetles developed I can do no better than give the counts made on a native tree September 6th, when nearly all of the beetles had escaped. There were on the tree and ground 2,541 plums, 795 of which bore 894 gouger marks and the number of exits was 234. If this tree was a fair test, and I judge from partial counts on many other trees that it was, it indicates that 26 out of every 100 gouger marks will produce mature insects.

REMEDY.

Treat as for plum curculio.

CUT WORMS.

The common brown cut worm is met with in every garden, and are familiar to everyone who has delved in the ground. They are one of the most destructive worms, to plants and vegetables. They live in the ground, but leave their places of concealment in the night to prey upon and devour vegetation. They are particularly partial to corn, cabbage and tobacco.

REMEDY.

Where cut worms have been hard on a field or garden, after preparing the field for crop, and where green food has been made scarce by the plowing of the land, a very successful way to exterminate is to cut green grass or weeds and scatter over the ground. Use at the rate of one pound of arsenical compound to ten gallons of hot water. Add to this liquid one ounce of London purple, then spray field; saturate the ground as well as grass, and you will get rid of them to a great extent. After the field has been sprayed with this compound, spray again with good results at intervals, using no London purple. Use ashes around plants, then saturate the hill; this will lessen their ravages. When you see the moth flying around, kill them, and you will kill what would have been followed by hundreds.

ROSE SAW-FLY.

The rose saw-fly is still another pest that is proving very destructive to the cultivation of roses. The fly is a shiny, black insect, appearing in the latter part of May and up to the middle of June, the female laying its eggs in incisions made by its saw into the skin of the leaf. The young, which appear in ten days, are greenish, almost transparent slugs, which are found in great numbers feeding on the foliage, causing it to look seared and burned.

REMEDY.

For saw-fly and all worms on rose bushes, spray with No. 10. Dissolve 1 pound in 4 gallons of boiling water. Stir till all the compound is dissolved. Add 6 gallons of cold water. Spray bushes with force pump at or about sundown. Repeat whenever these insects are to be found.

CHERRY AND PEAR TREE SLUG

These insects appear as a small shining black fly, one fourth of an inch long, in early and late summer months. They deposit their eggs on the under side of the leaves. The larvae are brown and tapering, with twenty feet or pedals. They are covered with an olive colored slime, hence the name slug. The larvae or worms feed upon the cuticle of the leaf, causing it to turn brown. In three weeks from the time of deposit, the slugs mature and pass down the tree into the earth, where they pupate, the flies of the first brood appearing in May and June. They are very destructive in their habits.

REMEDY.

Take air slacked lime, stand on the windward side of the tree, scatter the lime by means of a small shovel, or otherwise, so that the wind may carry the lime dust so as to light on the leaves of the tree infested. Hardwood ashes will answer in place of the lime. No. 10 used as for rose saw fly is a sure remedy.

GOOSEBERRY AND CURRANT WORM.

About the first of May a yellow fly, with black head, similar in appearance and in size to the common house fly, makes its appearance. It begins laying its white, transparent eggs on the under side of the leaves, which hatch in about four days green tweenty legged worms, which begin to feed on the leaves. They are voracious and grow rapidly, attaining three-fourths of an inch in length, when they go under the leaves or into the earth, or remain attached to the trees and spin their cocoons. The fly appears again in June or July, lays its eggs for a second brood of worms, which again devour the foliage.

REMEDY.

Treat as for cabbage worms.

APPLE MAGGOT.

This pest confines its ravages mainly to fall fruit, but frequently attacks winter apples, causing them to fall off the trees in great numbers. The same remedy used in the destruction of the codlin moth will apply to this insect, although some horticulturists think that by feeding the fruit to the hogs, they at the same time destroy the next seasons crop of worms. It is the loss of one year's crop of fruit.

REMEDY.

Spray as for codlin moth.

PLUM CURCULIO.

The plum curculio is a little brown beetle, which hibernates during the winter months, and is ready for active business in the early spring. It is active mainly in the night, hiding in the day under clods and dirt. As soon as the fruit is set it penetrates it sufficiently to insert its egg, the egg laying continuing until midsummer, when it remains in the tree, feeding upon the ripening fruit. The eggs soon hatch and the young larvae continue to bore into the fruit where the eggs were deposited. They resemble maggots and grow to maturity rapidly, the fruit attacked fall prematurely. They attack plum, cherry, apricot, peach and apple trees, but confine their greatest depredations to the stone fruits. The fruit attacked becomes gnarled and unfit for domestic use. Hoticulturists have found that by alternating rows of plum trees with rows of apples, the curculio will confine its operations to the plums, thus letting the apples grow to perfection, and giving their attention mainly to the plums.

REMEDY.

I have found that spraying with kerosene emulsion was good for the destruction of this insect. I have also found that London purple was of some good as a destroyer. Therefore I can well recommend my arsenical compound, from the fact that it is composed of both London purple and kerosene, with other insect exterminators equally as good. Dissolve one pound of arsenical compound to five gallons of hot water; stir with old broom till all is dissolved then add five gallons water, (soft water is best). For first spraying, spray as soon as you can see the blossom buds. For second spraying as soon as blossoms fall, and for third, spraying when the fruit is as large as small cherries. After this work is done you will have killed all sap-sucking insects as well as curculio.

CLOTHES MOTHS.

These insects are quite small and in color a pinkish yellow, with long narrow wings somewhat fringed with a velvety fuse. When these pretty little moths put in an appearance in your house, look out for your clothes, as their eggs are laid in all kinds of furs, woolen goods and clothing. After from 12 to 16 days the eggs hatch and are a small caterpillar of a pale color with 16 legs, which cuts its way through anything and everything it comes in contact with in the form of furs and woolen goods, doing damage in their line in the United States to the amount of hundreds of thousands of dollars annually.

The most successsful way to exterminate them is to take equal parts of Scotch snuff and cayenne pepper, mix, and dust your clothes, trunks and around the edge of your carpets. You had better set your husband's brother, or hired men, at this work, as it has a tendency to give one a dose of sneezing, but it is sure death to the insects. You may look for this moth any time in early spring, and to make sure, keep on the look out.

GREEN APHIS.

On the twigs of apple trees and at the base of the buds, very small, black, shiny eggs are deposited by the green aphis, or apple tree aphis. These eggs can be found in the winter, and can be destroyed at this season more readily. When the apple buds begin to expand in the spring, the eggs produce small lice which immediately take possession of the swelling buds and tender leaves, inserting their beaks in them and feeding on the juice. They are very prolific, reaching maturity in ten days and reproducing their species in equally short time. They increase so rapidly that they are enabled to take possession of a tree as fast as it leaves, buds and blooms. With the advance of the season they form wings and fly away to form new colonies and prey upon the life of other trees. When trees are infested with the green aphis, the leaves become curled back, the tips pressing against the twigs, forming a covering for the pests, protecting them from the weather. When cold weather approaches, male as well as female aphis are produced and a stock of eggs is deposited for another year's pestiferous crop.

REMEDY.

For winter—It is well, owing to the fact that the aphis deposits its eggs on the tender young branches, to cut back the tips of the limbs. Burn all that is cut off. Spray the tree with No. 14 compound, nine gallons of water to one of the compound; add lime as for borers. It is hard to get the medicine too strong for winter use.

For summer spraying.—If you know that you have had aphis the previous year, you are safe to spray in the spring; do so for the first time as soon as the leaves are the size of a mouse's ear. Watch the tender twigs, examine closely, and when you find lice, you are safe in spraying. When the leaves curl up, this is a sure sign of aphis. Spray with No. 14 compound, 9 to 10 gallons to one of the compound.

WOOLLY APHIS.

One of the most dangerous insects to apple trees in the United States, is what is commonly termed the woolly aphis. The color of the aphis is dark brown, the body being covered with white down, presenting a cottony appearance. It makes its appearance on all portions of the tree, but attacks principally the roots, branches and trunks. The leaves and fruit are generally unmolested by this pestiferous and industrious insect. Occasionally in the summer the mature insects crawl into the branches of the trees, where they remain and form colonies, in which form they are known as the woolly aphis or apple aphis. It is in this form that they attack the trunk and limbs of the trees. They are easily detected by the cottony bunches or clusters. There preference is for sweet bearing fruit trees, but they do not confine themselves to any one variety, their ravages extending to all varieties. Unmolested until the end of the season, they take possession of the infected trees, covering body and limbs until they present the appearance of having received a coat of whitewash. Investigation of the little clusters or patches will reveal the presence of the female aphis and her young. When the female has attained full growth, it is about a tenth of an inch in length, with oval form, black head and feet and dusky legs. The abdomen is yellow. In the summer the insects are devoid of wings, and the young are produced alive. Among the wingless specimens there is a small sprinkling endowed with small wings, but these have but little of the woolly substance upon them. They are dark and plump. The wings are double, the front portion being nearly twice the length of the hind narrow wings. In the fall season the eggs are deposited for the production of another generation of the pests in the spring. The insects have hardy constitutions, and endure the coldest seasons. The eggs can be seen only by the aid of a magnifying glass of considerable power. They are usually deposited in the crevices of the bark near the surface of the ground. If suckers are permitted to grow, the eggs are also found in these. When the young first come out they are covered with fine down, appearing like small specks of mold on the trees. They increase in size as the season advances, the fine coating becoming more apparent with increasing age. The sap of the tree furnishes old and young with nourishment. The punctures they make in the limbs saps the life of the tree, the limbs becoming gnarly and weak, while the leaves turn yellow and fall. Their ravages frequently become so great as to cause the death of the tree.

The enemies of the woolly aphis are spiders, ladybirds and syrphus flies. The spiders catch them in their webs and destroy them by thousands.

REMEDY.

If the trees are infested with woolly aphis, it is necessary to dig around the trunks at the base, and follow the prescription that is given in the treatment for old trees.

CABBAGE APHIS.

Keep a careful watch in your cabbage patch and as soon as you see the aphis, a green insect, commence spraying, using No. 1 compound, one pound to 14 gallons of water. Melt the compound in five gallons of hot water, then add nine gallons of cold water. Two or three sprayings will keep the cabbage clear of the pests.

PEACH TREE APHIS.

When fully grown, the winged female aphis in about an eighth of an inch long, with black back and dull green abdomen. The wingless female is a rusty red color, with the antenna, legs and honey tubes of greenish tinge, while the winged males are bright yellow, streaked with brown, and the honey tubes are black. The peach aphis begins upon the young peach leaves almost as soon as the buds open, and continue their work during the greater portion of the season, unless destroyed by insects or prepared emulsions. These insects crowd together under the peach leaves and sap the juices, causing them to thicken and curl. The leaves also become discolored and fall off prematurely.

REMEDY.

Spray as for green aphis. See directions for green aphis.

CHERRY TREE APHIS.

This is a black insect that makes its appearance in the spring on the leaves of cherry trees almost as soon as the leaves begin to expand. They are hatched from eggs that are deposited on the branches in the fall. They multiply rapidly and are extremely voracious, sapping the life of the tree and injuring the fruit. In the latter part of the fall, males are produced and eggs are deposited at the base of the buds and bark fissures for a new spring brood.

REMEDY.

Use the same remedy as for green aphis, although it may be necessary to use the emulsion a little stronger than for green aphis, be sure to put the medicine on to kill. Use No. 14.

PLUM TREE APHIS.

These insects when first hatched in the spring, are of a white color, with a tinge of green, but when they mature the green becomes deeper, while some become black with pale green abdomen. They are similar in appearance to the apple aphis and multiply their species with as great rapidity. They are found on the leaves of plum and prune trees in the early spring, and as rapidly as the leaves unfold they are taken possession of by these insects.

REMEDY.

This aphis is somewhat harder to kill, owing to the fact that they form a kind of downy substance on the leaves, and from the fact that they seem to lay flat on the leaves, seemingly holding fast to them. Therefore it is necessary to put the medicine on with considerable force. Use No. 14, as directed for green aphis.

THE HOP LOUSE.

The hop louse (*Phorodon humuli*) is one of the most troublesome insects that the hop industry of the country has to contend with. Many experiments and large amounts of money are expended yearly in endeavors to eradicate them from the fields. This insect lays its eggs in the fall. The eggs are glossy black and exceedingly small, and are hatched in the spring. They produce several generations in the course of the season, being as prolific as they are destructive. The female can produce over a hundred young, and each generation can reproduce in eight or ten days, so that they multiply by millions. It is estimated that ten generations are produced in the course of one season, and if left to their own course, will destroy, during the season, the labor of thousands of honest hop producers.

REMEDY.

Use No. 14 compound, one pound to from 10 to 12 gallons water. Dissolve in five gallons of hot water. Stir till all is dissolved, then add cold water. Spray as often as necessary to keep hops free from the insects.

CHICKEN LICE AND MITES.

If hens are infested, dissolve one pound of No. 14 compound in four gallons of hot water and stir till it is thoroughly mixed, then add five gallons of cold water. Take the infected fowls by the bills with one hand and by the feet with the other and douse them head first till thoroughly saturated. After this work has been performed, dissolve one pound of the compound in eight gallons of water, as above described, with the exception of the use of cold water, it should be used hot and enough lime put in to make a good white-wash, which should be applied to the coop, inside and out. Repeat this two or three times a year.

CATTLE LICE.

The same prescription as that prescribed for hens can be used on cattle or sheep. It destroys lice on cattle and scab on sheep.

REMEDY FOR MILDEW.

For mildew on grape vines and gooseberries, spray with winter wash and before the leaves come out, saturate the roots well. Spray with summer wash (No. 14, one pound to 10 gallons of water) immediately after the blossoms have fallen, and again when the leaves are full grown.

PLUM ROT.

The plum rot is caused by a fungus disease, which is destructive to all stone fruits. Very frequently the entire product of a tree is destroyed by this fungus, but it can very easily and cheaply be prevented by spraying with the Bordeaux mixture as well as the black rot of the plum and cherry, which disease is quite prevalent in many States. By adding London purple or Paris green to the above the curulico can be destroyed at the same spraying.

REMEDY.

Treat with the copperas compound, added to No. 14.

LEAF SPOT DISEASE OF THE PLUM AND CHERRY.

This disease causes injury to the foliage and at times inflicts considerable injury to both the plum and cherry, causing the leaves to drop prematurely, sometimes as early as the first of August, showing a spotted appearance. The same application as is used, Bordeaux mixture, to prevent plum rot will also prevent the leaf blight above referred to, and insure the trees a more healthy and thrifty growth.

REMEDY.

Treat with copperas compound, added to No. 14.

POWDERLY MILDEW OF THE CHERRY.

I have already in description of powderly mildew of the grape explained the peculiar character of this parasite, which is also injurious to the cherry, but can be easily prevented by spraying with the insect exterminator, No. 14.

SAN JOSE SCALE.

This is one of the most pernicious insects that has afflicted the Pacific coast. It not only attacks the fruit trees, but destroys the forest and ornamental trees as well. Its name is derived from the fact of it having first been discovered in the orchards of San Jose, where it was very destructive to fruit orchards. The full grown scale is about one sixteenth of an inch in length. The eggs are yellow, and the worms a pale yellow and very active, scarcely visible to the naked eye. They multiply rapidly, producing three broods in one season, and their presence on the trees is made known by the inner lining of the bark turning a reddish color. The fruit also becomes spotted in similiar manner, and shrinks and cracks open. The first hatching is in May, the second in July and the third in September.

REMEDY.

For winter treatment, cut back as far as the tree will bear, scrape all rough bark off the tree, then treat as for woolly aphis. Apply medicine to every part of the tree; don't miss a limb or twig.

For summer treatment, spray as for codlin moth. This is the worst scale that is to be found in the whole catalogue of the scale family, and great care should be taken in destroying them as the lease of life given to a tree or shrub is five years, after being once infested, if the scale is not destroyed.

OYSTER SHELL SCALE, COMMONLY KNOWN AS BARK LOUSE.

This is one of the worst scale insects that the eastern orchardists have to contend with, and was in all probability introduced into this country from Europe over 100 years ago. They don't confine their work of destruction to the fruit tree or shrub alone, as they are to be found on the hawthorne, and in fact I have found them on nearly all of the ornamental trees in some of the finest yards of Portland, Oregon. They are a sap-sucking insect; they live by inserting their beak into the bark of the tender growths, becoming so numerous as to obscure the bark from sight. In the fall these insects become simply a sack of very small eggs, and when in this condition their life mission is over. They fasten themselves to the twig or limb and become immovable, so far as the insect is concerned. In this state the insect dies and dries away, leaving the shell covering full of eggs (30-60) this shell covering making a perfect protection for the germ of spring.

REMEDY.

Spray in the fall or winter as for woolly aphis, using considerable lime. Trim as for old trees. Spray in the summer as soon as you can see the young scale in the form of specks on the branches. Spray three times during the season, 10 days between. Use No. 14 for summer and the arsenical compound for winter, as prescribed for woolly aphis.

PHYLLOXERA.

This insect is somewhat allied to the aphis and is subterranean in its nature. It commenced its ravages in the vineyards of France in about 1865, and since that time has baffled the wisdom of the most skillful horticulturists, to get rid of the disease. It has laid waste many of the finest vineyards, and, I am sorry to say, has put in its appearance in many portions of the United States, as I have experimented in its cure, both in California and Utah.

REMEDY.

If your vines are badly diseased, dig them up and burn them. Don't leave a vestige of rubbish in the ground, burn it likewise. If you conclude to try a perfect cure, which may be done if the vines are not too far gone, cut back the vines and then remove the earth around the base; scrape off all fungus growth as much as possible. After which treat with the same treatment as for woolly aphis, also scattering lime as for tomato blight.

BROWN APRICOT SCALE.

Adult Female.—Color, light brown. In shape resembles *L. hesperidum*, but is much larger and more convex. In the center of the dorsum is a prominent shining circular protuberance, from which radiate a number of small ridges; these are more noticeable upon the posterior half of the scale. From the convex center to the anus is a low carina, also noticeable in front.

Length, from .20 to .27 of an inch; width, from .12 to .15 of an inch; height, from .05 to .10 of an inch. Antennæ tapering to the point, seven-jointed; joints 1 and 3 subequal; joint 2 nearly three times as long as joint 1; joint 4 slightly longer than joints 5 and 6; joint 7 is nearly same as joint 3, and tapers to a point; a few bristles at the tip and upon each joint.

Eggs.—These are smaller and lighter colored than *L. oleæ*.

Larvæ.—Are long, oval, light yellow, darker down the center, and can be distinguished from the larvæ of *Oleæ* in not having the four reddish brown marks upon the dorsum.

I have seen these insects so thick on the apricot trees in California that they obscured the bark from sight, and the young larvæ were so thick on the leaves that a pin point could hardly be placed on the leaf without touching one of these little pests. They sap the very life out of the tree.

REMEDY.

Use same remedy as for San Jose scale.

THE RED SPIDER.

This pest is one of the fruit grower's worst enemies. It has, when full grown, the characteristic eight legs of spiders and is very small, only one sixty-fourth of an inch long. Its head partakes of a yellowish tinge. The female does not deposit her eggs, but when full grown attaches herself to a leaf and dies. Her skin protecting her eggs are then broken open by the male, exposing them, which soon change from colorless globules to a bright red. In size the egg is about the one hundred and fiftieth of an inch in diameter. The males may be seen busily removing the dead skin of the female, thus exposing the eggs to the sunlight. The young spider has only six legs, but in a few days sheds its skin and becomes eight-legged. The red spider devours the skin of leaves, buds and flowers, and covers them with a fine web, causing them to wither and die. When seriously infested the tree appears a dusky red, so numerous are the spiders. They begin their work on the soft portions of the tree, but finally spread all over. The wind blows them from tree to tree. One tree may be infested in still weather, but a constant wind will carry them in a stream across the orchard. They don't confine their ravages to the orchard alone; they sap the very life out of all kinds of floral shrubs and plants, being one of the florist's worst enemies. This insect is to be found scattered broadcast over this nation, as I have found them from the Atlantic to the Pacific. I have found as high as 50 trees dead in an orchard of from six to eight acres, not only in one state but many, and the owners did not seem to realize what was the trouble.

REMEDY.

For winter spraying, spray as for woolly aphis, as their eggs are hard to get rid of. For summer treatment spray as for green aphis.

Some of the most destructive insects that the fruit grower has to contend with have been so well described by Prof. Alexander Graw of California, that I cannot do better than quote him. The descriptions of the following insects are from a report of his to the State Board of Horticulture of California, while the remedies are my own.

FLORIDA RED SCALE.

This is a dark red scale, infesting citrus trees in Florida, settling on the wood, leaves and fruit. The scale of the female is circular, with the exuviæ nearly central. The position of the first skin is indicated by a nipple-like prominence, which, in fresh specimens, is white, and is the remains of a mass of cottony excretions, beneath which the first skin is shed. The part covering the second skin is light red, and the remainder is much darker, ranging from dark reddish brown to black; the thin part of the margin is gray. When full grown it measures .08 of an inch in diameter. The body of the female is nearly circular, and the color is white, with yellowish spots. The eggs are a pale yellow.

The scale of the male is much smaller than that of the female; the posterior side is prolonged into a thin flap, which is gray in color. The male is light orange-yellow in color, resembling the male of *A. aurantii*, but being smaller, having shorter antennæ.

REMEDY.

Same treatment as for San Jose scale.

FROSTED SCALE.

Description.—Adult female, pale brownish, thinly covered with a whitish powder, which does not conceal the ground color. Body oblong in outline, very convex above, not distinctly carinate, the surface very uneven. Margins nearly perpendicular; dimensions as follows: Largest specimens, length, .28 of an inch; width, a trifle over .20 of an inch; height, .12 of an inch. Smallest full-grown specimen, length, .16 of an inch; width, .12 of an inch; height, .08 of an inch. Antennæ much thickest at the base, 7-jointed; joint 6 the shortest, then 5, then 1 and 2, which are subequal in length; joints 3, 4, and 7 are also subequal in length, each nearly twice as long as 6; joint 7 tapers to the tip, and is furnished with a style, being about three fourths as long as this joint; anal cleft and lobes normal. The eggs are of the usual ovoid form of the *Lecaniums*, and of a yellowish white color, and are laid in May, June, and July.

Larvæ.—A few weeks after the eggs are deposited, the larvæ hatch out from under the old scale; they are of a pale color, having a distinct dorsal ridge extending the entire length of the body, and with many smaller ones (about twenty-four on each side) extending from it to the margin, some of them being divided into two branches.

The larvæ as soon as hatched locate upon the leaves; their development is slow until they take up their position upon the under side of the young shoots, where they remain throughout the winter, and, in fact, the balance of their lives. Upon the ascent of the sap in the spring they grow rapidly, and in April they assume the characteristic powdery or frosted appearance peculiar to this species.

REMEDY.

Exterminate as prescribed for San Jose scale.

CHAFF SCALE.

Scale of female is elongate, more or less oval, of a transparent brownish yellow color, and whitish near the border. The exuviæ are rounded oval in form, and are equal to about three-sevenths of the length of the fully formed scale. The scale of the male is light brown, with the exuviæ black.

Exterminate with the same treatment as for oyster shell scale.

LEMON SCALE.

This species differs from *Aspidiotus nerii* by the caudal lobes being more detached and more apparent, and by the plates being larger, and more particularly by the more elongated form of the last abdominal segment. The scale of the female is circular, yellowish white, with exuviæ central and yellow; that of the male is more elongated.

REMEDY.

Treat as for San Jose scale.

PURPLE SCALE.

This species can be very easily confounded with *Mytilaspis pomorum*, being very much like it in shape, but it is only found on citrus trees.

The scale of the female is long, slightly curved, and widened posteriorly. It is brown, with a purple tinge; the exuviæ brown, with delicate margin. Ventral scale is well developed and of a dirty white color. It is a single piece attached to the lower edge of the scale, and is more or less incomplete posteriorly. Length of scale, .12 of an inch. The color of the female is pale yellow. The eggs are white and placed irregularly under the scale.

The scale of the male is usually straight; of the same color as that of the female, sometimes almost black; the larval skin light yellow. For about one quarter of the length from the posterior end the scale is thin, forming a hinge which allows the posterior part of it to be lifted when the male emerges. Length, .06 of an inch.

REMEDY.

Exterminate with same treatment as for San Jose scale.

RED SCALE OF THE ORANGE.

This is a circular scale commonly known as the red scale, infesting citrus trees. This species resembles *Aspidiotus ficus* in shape, size, and the nipple-like prominence. The color varies from light greenish yellow to reddish brown. The central third is as dark, and usually darker, than the remainder of the scale, and when the female is fully grown the peculiar reniform body is discernible through the scale, causing the darker part of the outer two-thirds of the scale to appear as a broken ring. The female is light yellow in color in the adolescent stages, becoming brownish as it reaches maturity. When fully developed the thorax extends backwards in a large rounded lobe on each side, projecting beyond the extremity of the abdomen and giving the body a reniform shape.

The scale of the male is smaller than that of the female, and the posterior side is prolonged into a thin flap. The part which covers the larval skin is often lighter than the remainder of the scale. The male is light yellow, with the thoracic band brown, and eyes purplish black.

The eggs have never been seen excepting in the female's body, but larvæ having been found under the scale, it is supposed that the female is viviparous.

REMEDY.

Treat same as for San Jose scale.

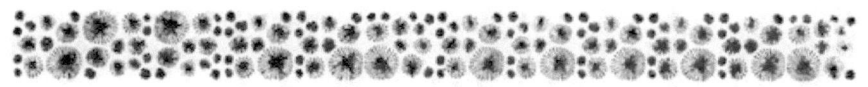

PART III

Remedies for the Insects That Destroy.

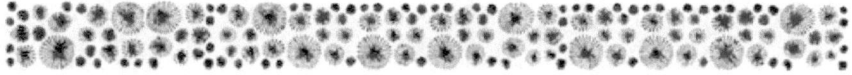

PROF. BROWN'S INSECTICIDES.

While it has been fully demonstrated that the "Prof. W. H. Brown's Insecticides" are the best, nevertheless I am aware of the fact that there are many others that have been recommended and used with good results. The most of which have been recommended either by the Horticultural department at Washington or the Provincial government at Ottawa, Canada, chiefly by Prof. C. V. Riley, Prof. Comstock and many other eminent men, and by State Boards of New York, California, Oregon and many others, also British Columbia. Therefore I have selected from the many receipts recommended and approved by all and have given them a worthy place in this department, hoping that if one proves a failure, that another, then another can be tried until the one that does the best work for the least money shall be found and used by the horticulturist, for which I feel greatly indebted to those who have so kindly contributed.

FORMULA FOR MAKING PROF. BROWN'S INSECTICIDES IN SOLID FORM.

[COPYRIGHTED 1894.]

FORMULA No. 10.—TOBACCO AND QUASSIA EXTRACTS.

Take two pounds of tobacco waste (or cheap tobacco) and three pounds of quassia (Oregon grape or wild sage will do), put into a boiler and boil till all strength is extracted. Boil the liquid down to two gallons of the solution. Pour liquid into a jar, label as "Receipt No. 10—Tobacco and Quassia Extract." Set this to one side and keep it corked.

Quassia and tobacco diluted one gallon to seven gallons of water is a very good rose aphis exterminator. It also may be used with good results on hot-house and green-house plants.

Formula No. 11.—Fish Oil, (Whale Oil or Dog-fish Oil, Dog-fish Oil Best.)

How to Make Twenty Pounds of Fish Oil Soap.

Take boiling water...2 gals.
Add to the boiling water, costic soda...................................5 lbs.
Then add Babbits' or Lewis' lye...5 lbs.

Pour the lye into the liquid slowly as the lye will cause the liquid to boil over if using small kettle. Take off the fire. Stir till all costic and lye have been dissolved, then set on a slow fire and let it come to a boil. Then mix one gallon fish oil and five pounds of lard together so as to be hot enough to pour in one body, and while stirring, slowly pour the lard and fish oil into the boiling liquid. Keep stirring till the whole becomes like froth. Stir till the froth settles and your soap thickens, looking, when done, like thick corn meal mush. Then your soap is made. Empty, then label and keep covered.

P. S.—All lye may be used in the making of Fish-oil Soap, but the use of costic soda and lye combined is better.

Dissolve one pound of Fish-oil Soap in 10 gallons of hot water. Add to this two quarts of Quassia and Tobacco Compound. This is good for the extermination of red spider and other sap-sucking insects. Make your own soap and thus save money.

Formula No. 12.—How to Make Creosote Compound (or Carbolic Acid, Creosote is Best.)

Take cold lard..5 lbs
Put lard into kettle, add to the lard, creosote (carbolic
  acid will do)..8 lbs.
  Stir till the lard and creosote comes to a boil.
Add to the lard and creosote, boiling water......................2 qts.
Stir thoroughly and add to this Babbits' or Lewis' lye.......2 lbs.

Stir, boiling by a slow fire, till this compound becomes like thick soap. Empty the emulsion into a jar, keg or barrel. Label and keep covered; then use as necessity may require.

FORMULA NO. 13.—HOW TO MAKE SULPHUR COMPOUND.

Take dry flour of sulphur (put into iron kettle..................4 lbs.
Then add to dry sulphur, Babbits' or Lewis' powdered lye..6 lbs.
Stir sulphur and lye together thoroughly after which pour
        into dry sulphur and lye, boiling water...................2 qts.

Before placing on the fire, stir slowly as the heat of the lye will cause the compound to boil over. After which set it on a slow fire and boil down till it becomes like a thick gruel. Empty, label and keep covered.

To make sulphur compound and arsenical compound for the destruction of the codlin moth, plum gouger, canker worm and other leaf and fruit eating insects, add 1 oz. red arsenic to dry sulphur and lye, mixing thoroughly together before adding water.

CAUTION.

Don't breathe the fumes while making arsenical compound.

How to Make Fifty Pounds of Insecticide, No. 14.

[This formula, No. 14, is the one over all others for which Prof. Brown claims, and justly, such excellence. Too much care cannot be taken in its preparation.]

CAUTION.

Be sure and have one thing fixed in your memory and that is, this Insecticide is finally made out of all the other formulas, namely, Nos. 10, 11, 12, 13, also kerosene. For instance, the first thing to do is to make No. 10, label and set aside. Next make No. 11, label and set aside. Next make No. 12, label and set aside. Next make No. 13, label and set aside. Then make from all these, Insect Exterminator No. 14, as directed in formula and you can't fail.

The first thing to be done is to put into the kettle, tobacco
        and quassia extract (See Formula No. 10).............2 gals.
    Let these extracts come to a boil on a slow fire.

Formula No. 11.

Add whale oil soap...20 lbs.
    Stir till all the soap is dissolved in the extract.

Formula No. 12.

Add creosote compound.. 4 lbs.
Stir till all is dissolved.

Formula No. 13.

Sulphur compound.. 4 lbs.
Stir on a slow fire till all is thoroughly mixed.

Formula.

Add kerosene oil (crude petroleum is best)............ .... 2 gals.
Stir till the whole compound becomes a very thick soap; remove the compound while warm into a keg or jar; keep covered tightly and use as necessity may require.

Copper Compound (Blue Vitrol)—To be added to No. 14, for Fungus Diseases Only.

Dissolve in two quarts of hot water, blue vitrol................... 1 lb.
Dissolve in two quarts of hot water, soda ash................. ½ lb.

After both are dissolved mix them together by stirring at least 30 minutes. Set aside and let settle over night. The copper will have settled. Pour off the clear water leaving the thick substance in the bottom undisturbed. Pour on water. 1 gallon. Stir 30 minutes and let stand still till all the thick substance has settled and the water has become clear. Pour off clear water as before. The thick substance that has settled to the bottom, take. In making sulphur compound, add this one pound, as directed in sulphur compound, which can be used in making No. 14 for the destruction of all fungus diseases.

The process of compounding the Copper and Sulphur Compound is the best known to chemistry, so as to get the copperas and sulphur to mix with water, and can be used in compounding any insecticide where copperas and sulphur are used.

C. E. BOGARDUS,
   ASSAYER AND CHEMIST.
     60 COLUMBIA ST.

CHEMIST FOR THE
Seattle Board of Health
CITY CHEMIST.

SEATTLE, WASH., August 21, 1894.

Prof. W. H. Brown, Seattle, Wash.:

DEAR SIR—I have carefully examined the formulas of your "Prof. W. H. Brown's Insecticides" and find them to be compounded upon thoroughly scientific principles for obtaining the different ingredients in the form of a solution or emulsion to gain the best results, especially the sulphur, arsenic and copper.

                                        Respectfully,
                                              C. E. BOGARDUS.

GROW YOUR OWN TOBACCO.

Tobacco being one of the chief ingredients used in the "Prof. Brown's Insecticide" therefore I would advise the growing of tobacco by every farmer, hop grower, gardener and florist, there being no necessity for consumer to buy tobacco from the fact that it doesn't require a good quality of tobacco for this purpose; therefore the tobacco used can be grown as easily as any other plant grown in the garden. I recommend that the consumer plant his own tobacco and save money by so doing.

OTHER REMEDIES RECOMMENDED.

1—ROOT INSECT.

One ounce of copperas to a pailful of water is sometimes effective in destroying root insects.

2—KEROSENE EMULSION FOR SMALL QUANTITIES.

Soft soap, 1 quart, or hard soap—preferably whale oil soap—¼ pound; 2 quarts hot water; 1 pint kerosene. Stir until all are permanently mixed, and then dilute with water to one-half or one-third strength. A good way to make the emulsion permanent is to pump the mixture back into the receptacle several times. Makes a permanent emulsion with either hard or soft water.

3—TO DESTROY CUT WORMS.

Put a teaspoonful of Paris green or London purple in two gallons of water and sprinkle handfuls of grass, green sods or other vegetation, which can then be scattered throughout the patch, walking crossways of the harrow marks. By doing this towards evening after the last harrowing, during the night the cut worms that are deprived of their food will be out looking for fresh pasture, and will appropriate of the prepared bait, the smallest particle of the poison of which will kill. If the worms are very troublesome, the remedy can be repeated, it being easily applied.

SHIELDING THE STEM.

By encircling each plant that is set with a piece of tar paper, or even other paper, the ravages of the worm may be prevented. The paper should extend upwards several inches from a point just beneath the surface of the soil.

HUNTING AND KILLING.

By closely examining the surface of the soil in the morning, in the vicinity of their spoils, through drooping plants or otherwise their place of retreat may usually be discovered, and the worms killed.

4—FOR THE DESTRUCTION OF PLANT LICE.

FORMULAS GROUPED AS FOLLOWS.

Tobacco—Used in the following ways:
1. Tobacco water, used with whale oil soap.
2. Dust.
3. Fumes. Burn dampened tobacco stems.
4. Nicotyl. Steep tobacco stems in water and evaporate the water.
5. Tea, or common decoction. Boil the stems or dust thoroughly, and strain. Then add cold water until the decoction contains 2 gallons of liquid to 1 pound of tobacco.

5—FOR FUNGUS.

CARBONATE OF COPPER IN SUSPENSION.

When the carbonate is to be used in suspension, instead of adding the ammonia to the sediment, add water until the whole quantity is made up to 6 quarts. Stir this thoroughly until the sediment is completely suspended (entirely mixed throughout) and pour the thick liquid into a suitable jar, when it will be ready for use. Before using shake the contents thoroughly, so that all the sediment may be evenly distributed in the water. Pour out a quart of the thick fluid and mix with 25 gallons of water.

6—FOR BLACK SCALE ON OLIVE TREES.

Directions for making emulsion:
Kerosene oil (150 degrees test)............5 gallons
Common laundry soap............1¼ pounds
Water............2½ gallons

After the above is emulsified, use by diluting one gallon of the mixture to six and one half gallons of water, and add two and one half pounds of home-made soap, dissolved in a little boiling water, to the solution (all the mixing is done with hot water), and apply at a temperature of 140 degrees Fahrenheit.

7—SUMMER WASH FOR SAN JOSE SCALE.

Whale-oil soap (80 per cent strength)............20 pounds
Sulphur............3 pounds
Caustic soda (98 per cent)............1 pound
Commercial potash............1 pound
Water to make 100 gallons.

Place sulphur, caustic soda, and potash together in about two gallons of water, and boil for at least one hour, or until thoroughly dissolved. Dissolve the soap by boiling in water; mix the two and boil for a short time; use the solution hot.

To accomplish the best results this wash should be used soon after the scales have hatched. From the middle of May until the beginning of July the great hatching takes place. Carefully examine the trees about that time, and after you are satisfied all are hatched apply the wash. It is very important to use a good quality of soap in the preparation of this wash. To test the soap spread five ounces of it on a tin plate and place it on top of a pot of boiling water. The loss in drying will indicate the amount of water in the soap. Thus, if one ounce is lost in drying, the soap would be of 80 per cent strength.

8—WOOLLY APHIS.

Root form.—**Dress** liberally with ashes, especially in moist localities, or use gas lime, about one and one half shovelfuls around each tree in such a manner that it will not come in contact with the bark of the tree.

Branch form.—Brush with kerosene emulsion or rosin solution, or spray.

9—FOR APHIS ON PRUNE TREES.

Caustic soda (98 per cent)	1 pound
Rosin	6 pounds
Water	40 gallons

Prepare as directed in rosin wash for winter use.

10—WINTER WASH FOR ALL KINDS OF SCALE AND FUNGUS.

The following formula and directions, if properly carried out, will produce an effective solution:

Unslacked lime	40 pounds
Sulphur	20 pounds
Stock salt	15 pounds

Water to make 60 gallons.

Directions.—**Place** ten pounds of lime and twenty pounds of sulphur in a boiler with twenty gallons of water, and boil over a brisk fire for not less than one hour and a half, or until the sulphur is thoroughly dissolved. When this takes place the mixture will be an amber color. Next place in a cask thirty pounds of unslacked lime, pouring over it enough hot water to thoroughly slack it, and while it is boiling add the fifteen pounds of salt. When this is dissolved add to the lime and sulphur in the boiler and boil for half an hour longer, when the necessary amount of water to make the 60 gallons should be added. This is an excellent winter wash for fruit trees.

11—PYRETHUM OR BUHACH.

FOR CURRENT WORMS ETC.

A tablespoonful of the pure powder to two gallons of water, applying it by sprinkling with a watering pot, or better yet, by force with a pump. Here, as in all cases where we use liquids to destroy insects, especially if, as in this case, it kills by contact, we must apply with great force, so that the liquid will spatter everywhere and so touch every insect.

12—KEROSENE EMULSION FOR ROOT INSECTS.

Professor Forbes has recommended that the roots of nursery trees be "puddled" with the kerosene emulsion before sending out, and that if the lice are seen upon the trunks, these be also treated with the emulsion, applying with a brush, sponge or cloth.

13—PARIS GREEN REMEDY FOR CODLIN MOTH.

For spraying apple or pear trees, use one pound of Paris green to two hundred gallons of water. It is best to first mix the poison with a small quantity of water, making a thick batter, and then dilute the latter and add to the reservoir or spray tank. By the addition of about two pounds of lime, which has been slacked and strained, there will be no danger of burning the foliage. Mix the whole thoroughly, and spray soon after the fruit has set, while yet in an upright position. At least two applications should be made, the second in about ten days. It would be still better to make three or four applications, at later intervals. For smaller quantities use a teaspoonful of Paris green to a pailful of water.

For early apples, do not spray later than the latter part of June. Very little benefit, if any, is received from spraying much later, even for late apples, as the egg, if laid in the side of the apple, is protected, and the moth is not reached by the spray in time.

The fallen fruit should be promptly gathered and destroyed. It has been recommended that hogs be kept in the orchard for the purpose of devouring such fruit, and where they can be so kept without injury to the trees or to the other crops, they will, no doubt, prove useful.

14—SUMMER REMEDY FOR PEARS AND APPLES.

Caustic soda (98 per cent)	10 pounds
Potash	10 pounds
Tallow	40 pounds
Rosin	40 pounds

Directions.—First—Dissolve the potash and soda in ten gallons of water. When dissolved place the whole amount in the barrel (fifty gallon measure).

Second—Dissolve the tallow and rosin together. When dissolved add the same to the potash and soda in the barrel, and stir well for five minutes or so. Leave standing for about two hours, then fill up with water, stirring well as every bucket of water goes in. Use the following day; one pound to the gallon of water; apply warm.

15—FOR PEACH ROOT BORER.

Remove the earth at the base of the tree and wrap up the trunk with stout paraffine paper, and pile up against the paper air-slacked lime or ashes.

16—BORDEAUX MIXTURE FOR FUNGUS DISEASES AND SCALE INSECTS.

(*a*) Dissolve sixteen pounds of sulphate of copper in twenty-two gallons of water; in another vessel slake thirty pounds of lime in six gallons of water. When the latter mixture has cooled pour it slowly into the copper solution, taking care to mix the fluids thoroughly by constant stirring.

(*b*) Dissolve six pounds of sulphate of copper in sixteen gallons of water, and slake four pounds of fresh lime in six gallons of water. When cool mix the solutions as above.

This formula requires fresh lime. Air-slaked lime, or a paste made by allowing freshly slaked lime to settle, contains a large percentage of water; consequently, if they should be combined in the proportions indicated, there would not be sufficient lime to decompose the copper.

17—SAN JOSE SCALE. SUMMER REMEDY FOR PEACHES.

Potash.. 14 pounds
Caustic soda (98 per cent)........................... 8 pounds
Lime, unslacked.. 5 pounds
Fish oil, polar or seal................................... 10 gallons

Directions.—First—Dissolve the soda and potash by placing them together in about ten or twelve gallons of water.

Second—Slack the lime in the barrel in two gallons of water; then add the fish oil to the lime and stir well until the lime and the oil have turned to a thick batter; then add the soda and potash, water boiling hot, and stir well with a dasher for five minutes or more; then leave standing for about four or six hours; then fill up with cold water. Do not pour in all the water at once, but about two buckets at a time; stir well as the two first buckets of water go in, to prevent lumps. Use the following day. Apply cold, one pound to the gallon of water. In dissolving it, do not boil; but weigh the amount to be used, place in a barrel, and on top of it pour hot water, about one bucket to every 100 pounds of material. After pouring in the hot water, stir lively with a dasher, until it is entirely dissolved; then reduce with cold water until sufficiently thin to pass through the strainer; then place in the tank and fill up with water; stir well, and it is ready for use; apply cold.

18—REMEDY FOR APHIS.

Coal tar fumes.—Burn rags, coated with coal tar, attached to a pole.

19—SIMPLE SOLUTION SULPHATE OF COPPER.

Dissolve one pound of pure sulphate of copper in twenty-five gallons of water. While this preparation has in a number of cases been used with beneficial results, its employment, especially when the foliage is young and tender, cannot be advised. For spraying the vines in spring, however, before the leaves appear, it will doubtless prove as efficacious as any.

20—FORMULA FOR A CHEAP KEROSENE EMULSION FOR SAP-SUCKING INSECTS.

Cheap kerosene	8 pints
Water	4 pints
Soap	$\frac{1}{2}$ pound

Dissolve the soap in the water and add, boiling hot, to the kerosene. Churn the mixture by means of a force pump and spray nozzle for five or ten minutes. The emulsion, if perfect, forms a cream which thickens on cooling, and should adhere without oiliness to the surface of glass. Dilute one part of the emulsion to twenty-five parts of water. A common grade of kerosene, which is good enough for this work, can be bought in most localities at eight cents per gallon by the barrel, and the soap used can be made for one cent per pound. This would make the batch given above cost eight and one-half cents, and diluted with twenty-five gallons of water to one of the emulsion would make thirty-eight and one-half gallons of wash. At this rate 100 gallons would cost twenty cents.

21—APPLE TREE BORERS.

Guard trees from infection by placing a shake or board on the south and west sides of the tree, which protects it from sunburn; or give a coating of whitewash containing some soap and sulphur. In removing a borer, smear the wound over with grafting wax.

22—WHALE OIL SOAP EMULSION, FOR MEALY BUGS.

One pound of whale oil soap to five gallons of water. For mealy bugs and similar insects. It will injure some tender plants.

23—WHITE HELEBORE, FOR THE EXTERMINATION OF THE CURRANT WORM AND OTHER INSECTS OF A SMALLER NATURE.

White helebore.—A light brown powder made from the roots of the white helebore plant (*Veratrum album*), one of the lily family. It is applied both dry and in water. In the dry state, it is usually applied without dilution, although the addition of a little flour will render it more adhesive. In water, 1 ounce of the poison is mixed with 3 gallons. Helebore soon loses its strength, and a fresh article should always be demanded. It is much less poisonous than the arsenites.

24—REMEDY FOR APPLE SCAB. HOME MANUFACTURE OF COPPER CARBONATE.

As the precipitated form of carbonate of copper is not always obtainable from druggists, directions are herewith appended for the easy preparation of this material at a cost much less than the usual wholesale price.

In a vessel capable of holding two or three gallons, dissolve $1\frac{1}{2}$ pounds of copper sulphate (blue vitrol) in two quarts of hot water. This will be entirely dissolved in fifteen or twenty minutes, using the crystalline form. In another vessel dissolve $1\frac{3}{4}$ pounds of sal soda (washing soda), using 2 quarts of hot water. When completely dissolved, pour the second solution into the first, stirring briskly. When effervescence has ceased, fill the vessel with water and stir thoroughly; then allow to stand five or six hours, when the sediment will have settled to the bottom. Pour off the clear liquid without disturbing the precipitate, fill with water again and stir as before, then allow it to stand until the sediment is settled again, which will take place in a few hours. Pour the clear liquid off carefully as before, and the residue is *carbonate of copper*. Using the above quantities of copper sulphate and sal soda, there will be formed 12 ounces of copper carbonate.

Instead of drying this, which is a tedious operation, add four quarts of strong ammonia, stirring in well, then add sufficient water to bring the whole quantity up to 6 quarts. This can be kept in an ordinary two gallon stone jar, which should be closely corked.

25—REMEDY FOR ORANGE SCALE.

Hard soap, ¼ pound; boiling water, 1 gallon; kerosene, 2 gallons. Churn or pump the ingredients vigorously 15 or 20 minutes. Dilute ten times when using. This is the Hubbard or standard emulsion for the scale of the orange.

Two ounces of balsam of fir added to the above appears to increase its efficiency, and it causes it to adhere to foliage better. One-half pint of spirits of turpentine is sometimes added.

26—ROSIN WASH FOR WINTER USE. REMEDY FOR SAN JOSE SCALE.

The following are the proportions of materials for the winter wash.

Rosin .... 30 pounds
Caustic soda (70 per cent)... 9 pounds
Fish oil .... 4½ pints

Directions.—Place the rosin, caustic soda, and fish oil in a large boiler, pouring over them about 20 gallons of water, and cook thoroughly over a brisk fire for at least three hours; then add *hot* water, a little occasionally, and stir well, until you have not less than fifty gallons of hot solution. Place this in the spray tank and add cold water to make the necessary amount. Never add *cold* water when cooking.

27—KEROSENE IN PURE STATE.

In pure state, kerosene is used as an insecticide upon many plants, with various results. It does not appear to injure the coleus, rose, grape, peach and pea, but does injure the potato, tomato and gooseberry and other plants.

28—FORMULA FOR MAKING FISH OIL SOAP.

Crystal potash lye..1 pound
Fish oil..2 pints
Soft water...3 gallons

A strong suds made at the rate of one pound of this soap to eight gallons of water will also be found a uniformly safe and satisfactory wash to use, killing the lice and not harming the vines. After standing three days, however, the suds will lose its efficacy.

29—REMEDY FOR HOP APHIS.

Quassia chips...8 pounds
Whale oil soap...7 pounds

The quassia chips are boiled in about one gallon of water to each pound of chips, for one hour. The soap is added while hot, and allowed to dissolve. This solution is then diluted with 100 gallons of water. Use with sprayer.

30—FOR CODLIN MOTH.

FOR EARLY RIPENING APPLES AND PEARS.

Spray once with one pound of Paris green to 180 gallons of water, when just out of bloom.

FOR FALL AND WINTER APPLES AND PEARS.

Spray twice; first application as above, second application with one pound of Paris green to 200 gallons of water. Use the Paris green without any addition, simply stirring the liquid continually and straining before using.

31—PROTECTION AGAINST THE CODLIN MOTH.

There are two modes of fighting them generally made use of—one is to prevent the hatching of the egg, or the killing of the young worm while working into the fruit; the other is the catching of the worm in traps as it is escaping from the fruit, or having the fruit eaten by the hogs as soon as it drops from the tree and before the worm escapes. The first mode is without doubt the most successful, and is also the least expensive. This is accomplished by spraying the trees with London purple or Paris green, using one pound of either to one hundred and fifty gallons of water. Paris green is a compound of arsenic and copper. It is a far more powerful poison than arsenic alone, and is not soluble in water, hence it will remain much longer on the trees. London purple is another arsenical compound. It is the residue from the manufacture of aniline dye, and contains lime, arsenuous acid and carbonaceous matter. It is soluble, more adhesive and less poisonous than Paris green. It is better to wet the powder thoroughly and make a paste before putting it into the vessel of water, that it may not form lumps. The liquid should then be strained, thereby removing the sediment that is in the London purple. Some have reported that the London purple burned the foliage. This, doubtless, arose from a difference in the strength of the London purple, and we recommend that care be exercised and tests be made before using, so that it shall not be too strong. The spray is caused by forcing the liquid, by means of a force pump, through a fine perforated nozzle, made specially for the purpose. The finer it is the less liquid will be required. The important thing is to scatter the spray on all the fruit.

32—FOR CUT WORMS.

It will be found to well repay the trouble and expense to place a band of tin around each cabbage or other plant at the same time of setting out. These may very easily be made by taking pieces of tin 6 inches long and $2\frac{1}{2}$ wide and bending them around a spade or broom handle so as to form short tubes. In placing them around a plant the two ends can be sprung apart to admit the plant, and then the tube should be pressed about half an inch into the ground. I have found this a useful means of disposing of empty tomato and other cans. To prepare these easily, they need only to be thrown into a bonfire, when the tops and bottoms fall off and the sides become unsoldered. The central piece of tin can then be cut down the centre with a pair of shears, and form two tubes. Wrapping a piece of paper round the stems of plants when setting them out will also save a great many.

33—CARBOLIC ACID AND SOAP MIXTURE.

One pint crude carbolic acid, 1 quart of soft soap, 2 gallons of hot water. Mix thoroughly. This wash is used for borers and for plant lice. Apply with cloth or soft broom.

34—FOR FLOWERING SHRUBS OR GARDEN PLANTS.

Whale oil soap (80 per cent strength)......$\frac{1}{2}$ pound
Water......1 gallon

Directions.—Dissolve soap by boiling water, and apply at a temperature of 100 to 120 degrees Fahrenheit.

THE GREAT DEVELOPERS.

I would be neglecting a duty did I close this book without a word of thanks to the obliging gentlemen representing the numerous great western railway companies with whom, in the pursuit of my inquiries, I have come in contact.

However we, as a people, may differ in our ideas of the general management of the powerful corporations called railroad companies, we will all admit that many of the garden spots of our country would to-day have been a mere wilderness were it not for the enterprising energy of the men who represent these vast concerns. Personally I am under many obligations for valuable information and specimens which have benefitted not only myself but thousands of others in various states. Railroads are truly called the "great civilizer" and they can be as justly termed "great developers." The magnificent stretches of country, specially adapted to fruit raising, to be found in this western part of our great nation, have been opened to settlement by the several railroad companies whose net work of steel climbs the mountains and sweeps through the valley of this "wonderland."

WASHINGTON.

Of the "Evergreen State" it is a difficult matter to speak fully in the small space at my disposal or without leaving myself open to the charge of "drawing a long bow." Washington is truly a "wonderland." Its vast forests and extensive mines are but a part of the natural resources of this state. The wheat of Eastern Washington or the great lumber, mineral and even fish industries of Western Washington must be left to others. It is of fruit—the luscious peach or the kingly apple, the strawberry which is found in perfection in Washington, or of the grapes and other fruits of the famous Yakima country, I would speak.

There is no limit to the field open to the fruit grower in Washington, east or west. I wish I had space to describe the Yakima country with its high altitude and magnificent climate, or to dwell upon the production of the Walla Walla Valley, where I might venture to say almost everything, except tropical fruits can be and are produced.

Almost all these celebrated points are reached by the Northern Pacific, and information, that can be fully depended upon, concerning this state can be secured at any time by addressing any of the prominent officers at St. Paul.

As a hop country Washington, with its next neighbor, Oregon, stands at the head of the column. The famous White River Valley and the hop fields of Yakima are too well known to need description.

Whatcom county, with its twenty-five hundred or more young orchards which are now coming into bearing, together with the great Nooksack Valley has been opened by the Great Northern, and its vast and varied resources brought within the reach of the people. The fruit grower will be amply rewarded for his toil in this section as there is soil to produce and climate to bring to perfection the most varied classes of fruit, so that few sections of country offer better inducements, while the enterprise of the Great Northern railroad company provides excellent shipping for products.

OREGON.

Oregon, joining Washington on the south, is a counterpart of that state in many respects. The Cascade Mountains run nearly north and south through both, making an Eastern and Western Oregon as well as Washington. There is the same distinction of climate and altitude. The vast wheat fields and stock ranges of Eastern Oregon, the wonderful growth and excellent flavor of the fruits of that part of the state are known almost everywhere, while the famous Willamette Valley, of Western Oregon, stretching for 300 miles in length with a width varying from 50 to 75 miles, can produce fruit enough, as well as other products, to feed millions. One must see this great valley to understand its richness or magnitude. It is almost an empire within itself and through its whole length the Southern Pacific and Willamette railroad winds, ready to carry the produce of the soil to the markets of the world or to bring to this vast garden the settler or tourist who may wish to enjoy or view its beauties.

Besides the Willamette there is the fertile valley of the Rogue River. In addition to excelling in the apples and kindred fruit produced, it is a question if better peaches are grown anywhere than in the Rogue River Valley. Oregon produces almost all standard fruits from apples to the numerous berries, and its extensive fruit lands are traversed as fully by the Union Pacific and Southern Pacific as those of Washington by the Northern Pacific and Great Northern, and the terms "U. P." and "S. P." are almost household words in the state.

IDAHO.

While the name Snake River Valley may not sound attractive, it is one of the most favored spots for fruit culture on this continent. Idaho is justly proud of the Snake River country. I have travelled a great deal and have examined, closely, a vast area of fruit lands, and I think that for peaches, grapes and the numerous varieties of small fruits, the section of the Snake River country from Lewiston to Rapera is the peer of the best. All the necessary conditions for success are to be found there and the excellence of the flavor is on a par with the beauty of the fruit. Here again the railroad takes a prominent place as a developing force and brings the people into touch with other parts of the country.

The vast country through which the Snake River runs south I did not travel, but from Huntington south-east, the Union

Pacific traverses a land which needs but irrigation to make it a paradise for fruit growers. The water is there in abundance, and the near future will probably see a perfect system developed.

Boise City is the centre of another splended fruit section of Idaho traversed by the Union Pacific, a spur being run from the main line at Nampa to Boise City.

UTAH.

Of Utah I am tempted to say a great deal. The admission of Utah to the sisterhood of states will doubtless bring in numerous settlers and I may venture to say that none who come with a willinguess to toil will be disappointed with the reward given for their labor. Utah is more vast and is better adapted to fruit raising than many people realize. From the great Salt Lake basin of the northern part of the state, to the favored "Dixie" of Southern Utah, the heart of the fruitgrower is gladdened with a territory and climatic conditions that will produce varieties of fruit from the ever popular apple to the orange. "Orange?" you say; yes, orange, as I am quite satisfied that fruit can be produced in Southern Utah, appropriately termed "Dixie." The mountain ranges of Utah furnishes the water. The land is ready to return "an hundred fold" the investments of the husbandman and to give great crops of splendid fruit for the planting and culture.

The Union Pacific, Southern Pacific and Denver and Rio Grande railroads have already provided a highway of steel to many parts of Utah and they are still pushing their way into new territory, bringing to the settler joy, and opening to the over-crowded cities of the East an Eldorado for the thousands who only need the opportunity to become farmers and fruit-growers. To those who are prone to favor the occupation I so dearly love, fruit growing, Utah offers a field I know will suit them. The railroad companies already mentioned will gladly give needed information of the country.

CALIFORNIA.

Golden California has been a name to conjure with ever since the gold discoveries of '49. While the gold fields first made California famous, it is by the fields of golden fruit she is best known now. California fruit is as standard as the No. 1 hard wheat of the Dakotas.

While all the natural resources of California have been there for untold years, it was chiefly through the enterprise of the Southern Pacific railroad company that their development was made possible. Sections of country, now like visions of paradise, have been brought from the wilds by the incoming of that highway of commerce, the railroad. It would bewilder one who has never seen the fruit fields of California did I attempt to describe them. They are so extensive, so varied. The crops produced by the grape vines of California would seem, if told to many of our Eastern brethren, like stories from the "Arabian Nights." These things have been recorded by abler pens than mine, and in words not at my command. California is just California and no words of man can say more of it as a fruit country.

ARIZONA.

Arizona is attracting considerable notice just at this time. I have intended to visit that territory for some time past and trust to be able to do so in the near future. For diversity of climate Arizona is well known, and with irrigation there should be, and doubtless would be, excellent fruit grown in profusion. The Southern Pacific and other enterprising companies see there is a great future for Arizona and will soon open it up more fully for settlement.

BRITISH COLUMBIA.

Our cousins to the north have a fine country which is rapidly coming into prominence. The Canadian Pacific railway, built at a tremendous expense across a difficult and sparsely settled country, brought the people of British Columbia into almost close contact with the eastern provinces of the Dominion. British Columbia produces excellent apples and pears and almost all the various members of the plum family thrive well, while small fruits are very prolific. The Fraser River Valley will be one of the noted fruit producing sections of North America, and to the Canadian Pacific railroad company the possibility of developing this fine country is due.

STATE BOARDS OF HORTICULTURE.

The states appointing State Boards of Horticulture have been amply repaid for the act. I have become conversant with the work of many of these bodies in the states where my researches and labors have brought me, and I can speak in the highest terms of their zeal and ability in almost every instance. It is encouraging to find men of earnestness and ability working to advance so important a part of the resources of the nation as Horticulture.

Without discussing the causes, the fact remains that our fruit industry is seriously injured by the swarms of insects to be met at almost every point, from the Atlantic to the Pacific. To combat these pests, and to advance the general interests of the fruit industry, is the mission of our state boards. Whatever we can do to assist these boards should be done. No man, or body of men, is infallible and all are, or should be, willing to receive or give information. To this end let us all scan very closely the insects we have to deal with in protecting our fruit, and become as familiar as possible with the many diseases our favorite trees and shrubs are subject to. By doing this we will benefit ourselves and obtain information which will enable us to annihilate these pests. All valuable information obtained in our researches should, in such manner as we think best, be brought into general use. In this work our State Boards of Horticulture will do their share.

TESTIMONIALS.

WASHINGTON TESTIMONIALS.

C. E. BOGARDUS,
 Assayer and Chemist.
 60 Columbia St.

    Chemist for the
   Seattle Board of Health
    city chemist.

      Seattle, Wash., August 21, 1894.
Prof. W. H. Brown, Seattle, Wash.:

 Dear Sir—I have carefully examined the formulas of your "Prof. W. H. Brown's Insecticides" and find them to be compounded upon thoroughly scientific principles for obtaining the different ingredients in the form of a solution or emulsion to gain the best results, especially the sulphur, arsenic and copper.

         Respectfully,
          C. E. Bogardus.

 Office of S. G. DEWSNAP,
Mining Engineer and Analytical Chemist
 19 Colman Building, Front St.

      Seattle, Wash., Aug. 20, 1894.
Mr. W. H. Brown, Seattle:

 Dear Sir—Last spring, at your recommendation, the trees in my yard were sprayed with a solution of your insect exterminator compound with the exception of ($2\frac{1}{2}$) two and one half apple trees, i. e., two apple trees were not sprayed at all and ($\frac{1}{2}$) one half of one tree only was sprayed. The trees that were sprayed were cherries, plums, prunes and apple trees and they have all borne good crops of fine fruit. We have not seen a single wormy cherry or a knotty plum so far this year. The two trees not sprayed it is almost impossible to tell what they are, for they are so covered with all sorts of pests. We had some fruit last year, but not nearly so good a yield and not nearly so good quality, many of the cherries being wormy and the plums and prunes falling off before ripening.

Will further say that last year we had almost no roses, because destroyed by aphis, red spider and worms, but from one spraying last spring the bushes were cleaned and we have had abundance of roses all this season. Without spraying I am satisfied that we should have had no good fruit or flowers this year.

Yours very respectfully,

S. G. DEWSNAP.

ROSS, WASH., August 14, 1894.

To Whom it May Concern: This is to certify that I have sprayed with the fungicides as recommended by the State Board of Horticulture of Washington and have found them very injurious to the foliage and of no benefit to the fruit whatever. I have sprayed with the fungicide recommended by W. H. Brown and find it to be of no injury to the foliage and of great benefit to the fruit. While I consider the whale oil and quassia emulsion the best destroyer for green aphis, I consider the "Prof. Brown's Insecticide" the best for all general purposes as an insecticide for the destruction of insects. Signed,

WILLIAM CRAWFORD.

FREMONT, WASH., August 14, 1894.

I do not hesitate to state that Mr. William Crawford, whose name appears in the foregoing testimonial, is a man of truth and veracity. His word where given is unquestionably good and he is one of our best horticulturists. Signed,

H. P. MILLER, M. D.

SEATTLE, WASH., Aug. 21, 1894.

Mr. W. H. Brown:

DEAR SIR—I feel it my duty as well as my privilege to inform you that the cherry trees you operated on for me last spring, and that I had given up to die from bleeding, are now cured and have put on a good growth. I consider that you have not missed your calling when you are called to be a physician of trees. My peach tree that was dying, and that you said had peach yellows, has recovered, it having put forth two feet of growth this season.

D. W. JACKSON,
Cor. of Weller and Bush Sts., Seattle.

SEATTLE, WASH., Aug. 21, 1894.

To Whom it May Concern: This is to certify that my rose bushes were being destroyed by rose aphis, which were so numerous that they covered the whole surface of the tender growths and that by one spraying with the "Prof. W. H. Brown's Insecticide," diluted at the rate of one pound of the compound to eleven gallons of the water, it killed 99 per cent. of all insect life that was on when the spraying took place. It is a pleasure for me to say to the public that this insecticide is all that Mr. Brown claims for it.

JOHN W. GILSON,
1206 Lakeview St., Seattle.

SEATTLE, Nov. 21, 1892.

To the State Board of Horticulture, and to all others whom it may concern:

We, the following members of the Board of County Commissioners, do hereby certify: That the county poor farm orchard of King county, Washington, was two years ago and for many years before that time, one of the worst pest infested orchards in the state of Washington. That in the fall of 1890 we employed Prof. W. H. Brown to treat this orchard with his "Insect Exterminating Compounds," and he so effectually exterminated the pests that the trees have regained their life and vigor and have produced abundant crops ever since his application of the exterminator, and have been free from all pests except in a few instances where the insects came from neighboring pest ridden orchards. We recommend Prof. Brown's Compound to do all that he claims it will do in exterminating insect pests.

       FRED GASCH, Chairman,
       W. H. TAYLOR, Treasurer,
   Members of the Board of County Commissioners.

          GEORGETOWN, Dec. 7, 1892.

 During the fall of 1890, Prof. W. H. Brown cleansed my orchard with his Insect Exterminator which caused an improved quality and increased quantity of fruit, besides greatly improving the condition of the trees. I cheerfully recommend its use by all owning orchards.

     JULIUS HORTON, Ex-Assessor of King county.

 With one application of Prof. Brown's insect wash, my whole orchard, of about two hundred trees, have been practically rid of these pests. I think I can safely say that to-day there are on the whole orchard not so many as were on one small limb when Prof. Brown began work on them. A single day's work will now finish the job already so well begun. The work is not expensive, the application kills the pests and at the same time, cleans off the moss, etc., from the bark and leaves it in a bright and healthy condition. In a word, Prof. Brown's work is a grand success.

 I have also examined and applied his system of combined Irrigation and Fertilization and am confident that it will be as successful in its results as have been his efforts in ridding the trees of their enemies.

        C. B. BAGLEY,
     Vice-President North End Bank, Seattle.

OREGON TESTIMONIALS.

Prof. W. H. Brown:

DEAR SIR—I have this day made a careful and thorough examination of the orchards and yards of A. H. Johnson, E. J. Jeffery and Jacob Kamm, that were cleaned and sprayed by you last fall, and I not only find the trees and shrubs free from all insect pests, but the trees and shrubs are in a healthy condition and are taking on a new growth. All of the trees and shrubs in the above orchards and yards were very badly infested with the San Jose scale and woolly and green aphis before being treated by you, so much so that I had thought it about impossible to reclaim many, if any, of them. I regard the wash used by you as very effective in the destruction of all insect pests, and most heartily recommend its use by all who have trees or shrubs infested with any insects injurious to them. I desire to thank you and those associated with you for the very effective and thorough work that you have done in our orchards and yards in ridding them of the obnoxious pests that have infested them.

Very truly yours,

E. W. ALLEN,

Sec. and Asst. Inspector, State Board of Horticulture of Oregon.

GRANT'S PASS, March 17, 1892.

This is to certify that I have seen Prof. W. H. Brown inspecting orchards for injurious insect pests, and have talked with him on subjects pertaining to infested orchards, and from my personal knowledge of Prof. Brown I would most cordially recommend to all the fruit men of Southern Oregon, who have the fruit interest at heart and desire the removal of any and all kinds of injurious insects and pests from their orchards, to avail themselves of Prof. Brown's knowledge. My faith is such that

I have bought of Prof. Brown his remedies for the suppression of injurious insect pests, so as to be prepared in the event should my orchard or nursery ever become infested.

A. H. CARSON,
Redland Nursery.

PORTLAND, Oct. 9, 1891.

To Whom it May Concern: This is to certify that the fruit trees and shrubs in my home orchard and lawn were terribly infested with insect pests, such as San Jose scale, woolly aphis, codlin moth, and in fact all other insects that fruit trees seem to be heir to. I engaged Prof. W. H. Brown, who operated on them with his Insect Exterminator, and I am convinced that he has left few, if any, to tell the story. I take pleasure in recommending him to the public, and also endorsing the testimonials given him in other states.

A. H. JOHNSON, Capitalist.

APPLEGATE, April 18, 1892.

Prof. Brown's Insect Exterminator wipes out the San Jose scale. I know this to be a fact for I have tried it.

W. B. YORK.

Postmaster Hammond, of Ashland, said to a *Tidings'* reporter: "I have about seventy trees, apple, cherry, pear, and plum, on my lot, and many of them were so badly infested with the San Jose scale that I had determined as a final resort to set fire to them. Prof. Brown, in looking over the various orchards about town, saw the condition of my trees and undertook to eradicate the pests with his Insect Exterminator. He applied the wash to all parts of the trees, and now instead of thinking of burning or cutting them down, I think they are entirely free from the pests that so completely infested them and will be as healthy as ever. Some of the trees were in blossom but the wash has not affected the blossoms in the least."

PORTLAND, Nov. 10, 1891.

To Whom it May Concern: I have been acquainted with Prof. Brown, intimately, for the past twelve years, and during all that time have known him to be an eminent man in his profession in the state of Minnesota; and from my acquaintance and knowledge of the man, can heartily recommend him as a trustworthy, reliable man, and a thorough expert in the care and wants of shrubbery and fruit trees.

W. H. JOHNSON,
Of the law firm of Johnson & Morcom.

PORTLAND, June 14, 1892.

My orchard was infested with San Jose scale, oyster shell scale, woolly and green aphis, to such an extent that I had lost all hope of eradicating them, when Prof. W. H. Brown called on me and asked permission to try his Insect Exterminator on my orchard. The test was so successful that I employed him to clear my orchard of the above pests, and I must say that he made a complete and clean job of it. I have no hesitancy in recommending him and his Insect Exterminator to all fruit growers, as his remedies are better than any of the California remedies that I have tried. In fact the Exterminator does all that is claimed for it to do.

JOHN MOCK.

CALIFORNIA TESTIMONIALS.

SANTA CLARA, July 1, 1892.

I hereby certify that Prof. W. H. Brown sprayed a prune tree that was badly infested with brown apricot scale, hatched and on the leaves. His spray, whatever it might be, began to show its effects as soon as dry. After three days, I have this day examined many leaves and do not find a live scale. One twig on another tree, all of which was affected with the live scale on the leaf, was sprayed and the same results found on the leaves of that twig. The woolly and rose aphis immediately yielded to his treatment.

Very Respectfully, Etc.,
PHILO HERSEY,
President West Side Fruit Growers' Association,
Santa Clara Valley.

SANTA CLARA, July 1, 1892.

To Whom it May Concern: This certifies that Prof. W. H. Brown has sprayed several trees of mine with a liquid preparation of his to destroy the plum aphis. I can say that all insects that were reached by the spray were killed. He has also treated an apple tree for woolly aphis. As far as such came in contact with insects the same were killed.

A. BLOCK,
Commissioner State Board of Horticulture,
San Francisco District.

SAN JOSE, July 2, 1892.

The orchards in the vicinity of San Jose are subject to the ravages of many insect pests so common throughout the state.

I have visited many of them with Prof. W. H. Brown and witnessed him experiment with his Insect Exterminator on the San Jose, brown and black scale, codlin moth and the woolly and green aphis. The insects were destroyed with one spraying, without injury to the tree or its foliage. From what I saw I am satisfied that this is the best insect exterminator ever introduced in this county, and should be used by every orchardist that cares to destroy these insects and preserve the orchards.

GEO. W. WELCH.

WATSONVILLE, July 20, 1892.

Prof. W. H. Brown:

DEAR SIR—The apple trees which you sprayed in my orchard with your Insect Exterminator, five or six days ago,—one being full of woolly aphis and the other having both woolly and green aphis on it—are now entirely clean and free from these insects. There is no perceptible injury to the foliage. One of these trees had been previously sprayed with the resinous preparation, but failed to destroy the aphis. I think your Insect Exterminator is the best I have ever seen, as it can be used at any time without injury to the foliage of the trees, nor is it harmful in any way to those who use it.

Yours truly,
JAMES WATERS.

Prominent orchardist and owner of Pajarro Valley Nursery.

WATSONVILLE, July 19, 1892.

This is to certify that Prof. W. H. Brown sprayed one tree of mine that was white as snow with woolly aphis. The insects were destroyed with one spraying without injury to the tree. I consider Prof. W. H. Brown's preparation to be the best woolly aphis exterminator I have seen.

S. MARTINELLI.

WATSONVILLE, July 19, 1892.

This certifies that Prof. W. H. Brown's Insect Exterminator is, in my estimation, the only one that will kill the woolly aphis, which is the hardest of all insects to destroy. It will also kill all other aphis and scale of every kind in five minutes; and in proof of what I say I have bought the county right of Santa Cruz county, which shows what I believe about the value of it as an insect exterminator.

W. H. BOWMAN,
Fruit grower and Nurseryman, Prop. of Corralitos Nursery.

WATSONVILLE, July 19, 1892

From actual observation I freely assert that Prof. W. H. Brown's Fruit Pest Exterminator and system of application is the safest and most effective of any I ever saw.

Respectfully,
A. N. JUDD.

WATSONVILLE, July 12, 1892.

This is to certify that Prof. W. H. Brown sprayed some trees in my orchard, using his exterminator. He successfully destroyed the woolly and green aphis. He also did some spraying on a tree that was infested with apricot scale, and wherever the Exterminator reached the insects they appeared to be destroyed.

J. A. McCUNE,
Horticultural Commissioner.

WATSONVILLE, July 19, 1892.

W. H. Brown's Insect Exterminator destroys woolly aphis to my satisfaction wherever it touches them.

M. B. TUTTLE.

WATSONVILLE, July 20, 1892.

I hereby certify that after being out in the various orchards in our valley the past week with Prof. W. H. Brown, and having seen the workings of his Exterminator, I do not hesitate to say that it is the most wonderful remedy ever applied to a tree or shrub, having seen it destroy woolly aphis, green aphis, plum aphis, codlin moth, black and brown scale, and hop lice in trees that had been washed with exterminators such as salt, sulphur and lime, rosin wash, I. X. L., and other exterminators such as have been used and recommended throughout our state, and had failed to exterminate—his remedy killing instantly, and leaving the tree and foliage in a good clean and healthy condition.

G. W. SILL.

WATSONVILLE, July 20, 1892.

I am willing to vouch for the truth of all the testimonials from Watsonville.

H. S. FLETCHER,
Cashier of the Bank of Watsonville.

IDAHO TESTIMONIALS.

LEWISTON, July 24, 1891.

To Whom it May Concern: To-day Prof. W. H. Brown has operated on my orchard for the purpose of showing what he can do in the way of destroying the scale and other insects which have such a strong hold on the orchards in this vicinity. I can say I am perfectly satisfied his recipes in connection with his Patent Irrigator and Insect Exterminator will destroy *every form of the insect pest*, if used as he directs. I am also satisfied the Professor has found the cause of so many tomatoes dying, and am thoroughly convinced that the recipe he will furnish, if properly used, will prevent death of the vine and cause them to produce a bountiful crop of fruit. I consider this alone to be well worth the price of all. I have purchased of him his Recipes and the right to use them, and his Patent Irrigator and Insect Exterminator.

Respectfully,
August Delsol.

Lewiston, July 24, 1891.

To Whom it May Concern: Prof. W. H. Brown visited my place yesterday for the purpose of making a personal examination of my orchard. I decided at once to have him operate. Am well pleased with his mode of operation, and thoroughly satisfied he can do all he says he can do. Without doubt, his Recipes in connection with his Patent Irrigator and Insect Exterminator will destroy every form of insect that infests our fruit trees. I consider it the duty of every one who has an orchard, to procure at once the best method of ridding it of the terrible pests that will so soon destroy not only their own orchards, but those of the entire country. So thoroughly satisfied am I that Prof. Brown has this, I have purchased of him an orchard right for his Patent Irrigator, Insect Exterminator, and his Recipes.

Respectfully,
Louis Delsol.

Lewiston, July 25, 1891.

To Whom it May Concern: Prof. W. H. Brown operated on a tree for me that was apparently in its last stages. In five minutes after the application of the liquid, every form of insect was dead. Four days after the operation, I find the foliage has returned to its natural color and new growth has actually put out.

The saving of this tree alone is worth more than the price of all. Every one who has an orchard, should have Prof. Brown's Recipes, and his Irrigator and Insect Exterminator.

James Kearny,
Henry McNaley.

LEWISTON, July 31, 1891.

To Whom it May Concern: By my request, Prof. W. H. Brown operated in my orchard for the extermination of the scales. So thorough and successful was his work, I take pleasure in recommending him to all fruit growers, trusting they will do as I have done—purchase his Recipes and his Patent Irrigator and Insect Exterminator.

JUDGE J. W. POE.

COLORADO TESTIMONIALS.

DENVER, April 15, 1893.

"*Resolved,* That the thanks of the Colorado State Board of Horticulture be extended to Professor W. H. Brown for his able and instructive lecture on injurious insects and for practical lessons in entomology, exemplified by practical labor and illustrations in the orchards of Jefferson county; that in the composition of Professor Brown's Insecticide we recognize the best and most effective remedial agents, and believe the Insecticide to be a safe and valuable remedy."

Signed: Judge W. B. OSBORN, President, Loveland.
JOHN TOBIAS, Secretary, Denver.
C. W. STEELE, Grand Junction.
DAVID BROTHERS, Wheat Ridge.

DE BEQUE, April 17, 1893.

To Whom it May Concern: I have visited many of the orchards in this vicinity in the past few days in company with Professor W. H. Brown and have seen him operate on the woolly aphis, red spider and brown scale with his Insect Exterminator and I have no hesitation in saying that his Exterminator is sure death to fruit pests. I have purchased the right to use it and believe it to be to the interest of all fruit growers to do the same.

WILLIAM HARRIS, Merchant.

GRAND JUNCTION, April 19, 1893.

I hereby certify that after being in various orchards in our valley the past week with Professor W. H. Brown and having seeing the work of his Exterminator, I do not hesitate to say that after seeing him operate on the green aphis, woolly aphis and red spider that his Exterminator is a success and that I have faith enough in it that I have purchased the right of western Colorado.

A. A. MILLER,
President, Grand Junction Fruit Growers' Association.

GRAND JUNCTION, April 19, 1893.

This is to certify that Professor W. H. Brown sprayed some trees in my orchard, using his Exterminator. He successfully destroyed the woolly aphis and green aphis and also the red spider, and I cheerfully recommend its use by all fruit growers.

ROBERT ORR,
Fruit Grower, Grand Junction, Colorado.

BESSMER, April 26, 1893.

I take pleasure in stating that I have tried Professor Brown's Insecticide and find it does the work satisfactorily, as far as greenhouse insects are concerned, and that I have purchased the right to use the formula.

HARRY BAKER,
Florist and Market Gardener.

CANON CITY, April 25, 1893.

To Whom it May Concern: This is to certify that I have visited several orchards in the neighborhood of Canon City in the last few days in company with Professor W. H. Brown, and have seen him operate on the woolly aphis and red spider with his Insect Exterminator, and have no hesitancy in saying it is just what we want in Colorado to exterminate the fast increasing insect pests in this state. This Insect Exterminator, as far as I have seen, will do all he claims for it. To show our faith in the same we have bought the right to use it for Fremont county.

JOHN GRAVESTOCK,
President of Fremont County Horticultural Society.

CANON CITY, April 25th, 1893.

To Whom it May Concern: This is to certify that I have seen Professor W. H. Brown exterminate orchard insects with his Insect Exterminator, and have such confidence in its efficiency in exterminating insect pests that I have purchased a one-half interest in Fremont county for his patents for the extermination of insect pests.

W. A. HELM,
Treasurer of Fremont County Horticultural Society.

UTAH TESTIMONIALS.

SALT LAKE CITY, May 27th, 1893.

To Whom it May Concern: I this day saw Prof. W. H. Brown operate on the woolly aphis, peach aphis, and the tent caterpillar, with his Insect Exterminator. The insects were alive and active upon trees as shown to me, but after being sprayed by the Professor with his exterminator, no signs of life were to be observed with the most powerful glass through which I looked.

Under these circumstances I have no hesitancy in indorsing the recommendations of Mr. George B. Wallace and Mr. John H. White.

ANGUS M. CANNON,
President Salt Lake Stake of Latter Day Saints.

SALT LAKE, Oct. 2, 1893.

Prof. W. H. Brown:

DEAR SIR—Do you know that your Insect Exterminator is the best bed bug exterminator I ever saw.

S. HALES.

GRANGER, May 18th, 1893.

To Whom it May Concern: This certifies that Prof. W. H. Brown sprayed fruit trees of mine for woolly aphis, tent caterpillar and cottony Cushing scale, with a liquid prepared by him for the destruction of insects. All insects reached by the spray were killed.

I fully endorse Prof. Brown's Insect Exterminator.

GEORGE B. WALLACE.

SALT LAKE, May 17th, 1893.

To Whom it May Concern: This is to certify that I have examined (to-day) several specimens of bark and twigs taken from fruit trees in our city, and found them fully alive with insect life, and that I witnessed Prof. W. H. Brown experiment with his "Insect Exterminator" upon the same, and the insects were immediately destroyed. I believe that Prof. Brown's remedy is sufficient to cleanse our trees from the pest of insects, and should be used by every orchardist who cares to preserve his orchard.

JOHN H. WHITE.

SALT LAKE, April 3, 1893.

This is to certify that in my presence Prof. W. H. Brown sprayed some bark and knots of fruit trees that were terribly infested with San Jose scale and woolly aphis, destroying all insect life with his Insect Exterminator in a few minutes.

M. CHRISTOPHERSON.
JOHN GABBOTT,
Salt Lake Nursery.

SALT LAKE, April 3, 1893.

Having had like experience with Prof. Brown's Insect Exterminator, I can, and do not hesitate to, endorse the above statement of Messrs. Christopherson and John Gabbott.

J. W. CHAMBERLIN & SONS,
Star Nursery Co.

NEBRASKA TESTIMONIALS.

HICKMAN, August 12, 1893.

To Whom it May Concern: Having purchased two bills of trees of Prof. W. H. Brown, 14 years ago, and having been much benefitted by his advice as regards sickly fruit trees and having now heard him explain the cause of the ruin the blight is bringing to our orchards, and having seen him operate with his Insect Exterminator on the tent-caterpillar, woolly aphis, codlin moth and cabbage worm, the exterminator killing instantly all insects that it came in contact with, therefore I have no hesitancy in saying that I have purchased an orchard right, and would unhesitatingly recommend its use to my friends and the public at large. J. STEIN, Fruit Grower.

MINNESOTA TESTIMONIALS.

ST. PAUL, MINN., October 4, 1889.

Prof. W. H. Brown. St. Paul:

DEAR SIR—Last June the four large hard maple trees in front of my house were apparently dying, when your apparatus was applied. Since then the trees have regained vigor, produced new growth and are evidently out of danger. I heartily recommend your apparatus to anyone similarly situated, or who is in danger of losing his shade trees.

A. W. KRECH,
Nat. Ger. Am. Bank Bldg., St. Paul, Minn.

State of Minnesota,
Executive Department.

ST. PAUL, October 4, 1889.

To Whom it May Concern: I am pleased to recommend Prof. Brown's Tree, Shrub and Lawn Fertilizing Apparatus as an appliance that accomplishes excellent results in the preservation of trees and shrubbery, and in producing a healthy growth. The apparatus was applied to trees upon the Capitol grounds, and the results are very satisfactory.

W. R. MERRIAM, Governor.

ST. PAUL, October 19, 1889.

I take pleasure in endorsing Gov. Merriam's recommendation of Prof. Brown.

COL. W. P. CLOUGH,
Vice Pres. Great Northern R. R. Co.

The trees on the Capitol grounds were, to all appearances, in a dying condition. The treatment given them by Prof. Brown has been most beneficial, causing them to put forth new foliage and infusing new life and vigor to those trees receiving his care.

W. W. BRADEN, State Auditor.

ST. PAUL, October 18, 1889.

I cordially endorse the statements made herein by Gov. Merriam, Auditor Braden and Col. Clough.

GEN. GEO. L. BECKER,
State Railroad Commissioner.

ST. PAUL, MINN., October 5, 1889.

Anyone who does not believe in Prof. Brown's Tree, Shrub and Lawn Fertilizing Apparatus can examine my tree on corner of Summit avenue and St. Peter street, where they will find a tree that had lost most of its foliage in August. Since that time it got a new coat of foliage, and has produced a vigorous growth.

E. N. SAUNDERS.

ST. PAUL, MINN., October 5, 1889.

To Whom it May Concern: I do not hesitate to recommend to the public Prof. Brown's Tree, Shrub and Lawn Fertilizing Apparatus from the fact that I had two large trees in a dying condition that I could hardly replace for money. Mr. Brown operated on them with his Fertilizing Apparatus. The trees are both in a healthy condition, one of which being the last to give up its green foliage this autumn.

GEO. PALMES,
260 Summit Avenue.

ST. PAUL, MINN., October 5, 1889.

I wish to state that one of the trees on the Capitol grounds, operated on by Prof. Brown, was in a dying condition at the time of the operation and had lost most of its foliage. It has reproduced a new foliage and growth, some of which being eight inches in length, and produced in sixteen days from date of operation.

C. A. ROSE, Janitor State Capitol.

ST. PAUL, MINN., October 5, 1889.

To Whom it May Concern: I have a tree the leaves of which turned yellow in August of this year. Mr. Brown put one of his Tree, Shrub and Lawn Fertilizing Apparatus to its roots, after which the leaves that were then on fell off, but soon reproduced new foliage, which was without a question, produced by Prof. Brown's Tree, Shrub and Lawn Fertilizing Apparatus.

GEO. BENZ,
5 Sherburne Avenue.

St. Paul, October 18, 1889.

I am fully satisfied that the applications as made by W. H. Brown, through his Fertilizer will save the life of trees, etc., to which they may be applied.

B. W. Brunson,
Prop. Brunson's Addition to St. Paul.

ST. PAUL REFERENCES BY PERMISSION.

Ex-Mayor Smith
Judge Chandler
Judge Gilfillan
Gen. J. H. Bishop
Gen. H. H. Sibley
G. H. Moffett
Hon. H. A. Castle
Hon. Wm. A. Van Slyke

Rt. Rev. Archbishop Ireland.
Ex-Gov. Alex. Ramsey
Sisters of St. Joseph Academy
Gen. Geo. L. Becker
Sisters of Convent Visitation
Ex-Gov. Marshall
Uri L. Lamprey
Hon. E. F. Drake

BRITISH COLUMBIA TESTIMONIALS.

New Westminster, Feb. 28, 1893.

To all Whom are Concerned: I beg leave to state that I have enquired as to W. H. Brown's Insect Exterminator, while in Oregon and find that I can cheerfully recommend its use to all owning orchards.

E. Hutcherson,
Inspector of Fruit Pests.

Victoria, Jan. 17th, 1893.

To Whom it May Concern: The trees on my place (Henry King's, corner Cedar Hill and Mt. Tolmie Roads) were almost alive with insects peculiar to fruit trees. Mr. Brown cut twigs from the worst of them, applied his mixture in my presence, and in less than five minutes thereafter, what was insect life assumed the shape of jelly, and the twigs were left clean of live pests. The experiment was a very interesting one. I have purchased his receipt for my own use.

Munroe Miller.

Having had like experience with W. H. Brown's Insect Exterminator, we can, and do not hesitate to indorse the foregoing statement of Munroe Miller.

JAMES TOD & SON,
DEANS BROS.

VICTORIA, Jan. 9th, 1893.

To Whom it May Concern: My fruit trees have been infested so that some of them were fairly covered with insects and eggs. A single tree had tens of thousands, almost beyond estimate. With one application of W. H. Brown's Insect Exterminator I can safely say there are few, if any, left to tell the story. I recommend W. H. Brown's Insect Exterminator to do all that he claims it will do in exterminating insects.

H. SAUNDERS, Merchant.

PRESS OPINION.

Prof. Brown showed us how to kill "chicken mites" with his insect exterminator this morning. The Professor got a board, literally covered with those insects, and sprayed it before a number of spectators, among whom was the Hon. David Stoker, and at the same time offering ten cents for each insect they could find alive in ten minutes after the remedy had been applied, but no one asked the professor for a reward.—*Davis County (Utah) Clipper*, March, 1894.

Can the blight on fruit trees be cured? Read what the *Colorado Field and Farm*, of Sept. 14, 1893, has to say on the subject:

"The science of tree doctoring may in time become a recognized occupation among horticulturists. Professor Brown, of Seattle, Washington, is in the business exclusively and during a visit to Denver last April he applied some remedial measures to a Wealthy apple tree in the orchard of David Brothers on Wheat Ridge. This tree was nearly dead from three year's attack of blight. To-day it is thrifty and apparently recovered from its recent illness. Its new growth of twigs measure over two feet and the tree is saved, whereas it would surely have been dead by this time but for Dr. Brown's treatment."

This experiment took place in the orchard of David Brothers, Wheat Ridge, who is one of the State Board of Horticulture of Colorado.

PHYSICIAN OF TREES.

There are doctors in Seattle for every ill that flesh is heir to, as everybody knows, but everybody does not know that this city can boast of a physician for the vegetable kingdom. Yet such is the case, and many are the owners of drooping and dying trees who have gone to him for treatment for their leafy friends and found comfort. His name is Professor W. H. Brown, and he came here from St. Paul about a year ago, having there restored to life and health many a sickly tree, just as a physician brings back the roses to the cheeks of a human patient.

Mr. Brown is a horticulturist, better described as a physician of trees. When he sees a tree drooping he examines it and finds out what the trouble is. He prescribes for a tree just as an ordinary physician would prescribe for a human being, and he has been almost invariably successful in saving their lives.

Professor Brown has treated the trees in the puplic parks of St. Paul which were being slowly killed by worms. He found 13 different kinds of worms, belonging to a family of 360 varieties. These worms get into the trees through the cracking of the bark by the alternate thawing and freezing in the winter. The sap oozes into the opening and forms a jelly in which the beetles deposit their eggs. The eggs hatch, the grubs devour the sap and then explore the tree in search of more. The same result follows the improper trimming of trees, when the wound is left uncovered.

Professor Brown has a method of treating trees thus afflicted which infallibly kills the insects and heals the wound which they have made. The results of his treatment are perceptible almost as soon as it has been given, and the patient soon shows its appreciation by displaying a bright green, healthy foliage. Another treatment is adopted with the insects which attack the leaves of a tree, and with equal success. Professor Brown has a method of feeding trees which suffer from lack of nourishment through being planted in a hard sidewalk.

If proof is needed that Prof. Brown is not a mere theorist, it suffices to say that he has practiced as a horticulturist for fifteen years and during that time has never had a failure. Since his coming to Seattle he has treated the orchards of a number of leading citizens of Seattle and King county.—*Seattle Post-Intelligencer*, April 7, 1891.

NO. 1

Forest tree Tent Caterpillar, perfect Moth with egg cluster on limb as shown in cut No. 1.

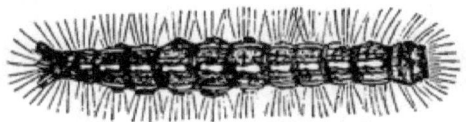

NO. 2

Worm produced from the egg of the Forest Tree Tent Caterpillar as shown in cut No. 2.

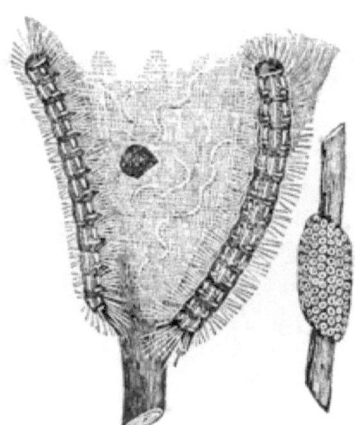

NO. 3.

Caterpillars produced from the eggs of the Apple Tree Tent Caterpillar, as shown on Tent in cut No. 3.

NO 4.
The perfect Codlin Moth and the worm produced from the egg of the Moth as it comes out of the apple.

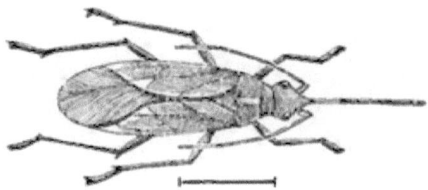

NO. 5
Box Elder Bug.

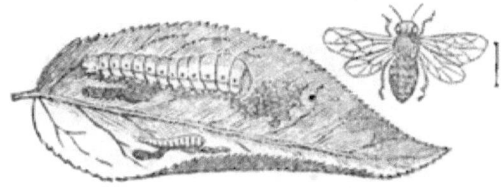

NO. 6
Showing the Perfect Cherry Tree Saw Fly and the Larvæ produced from the Fly on the leaf.

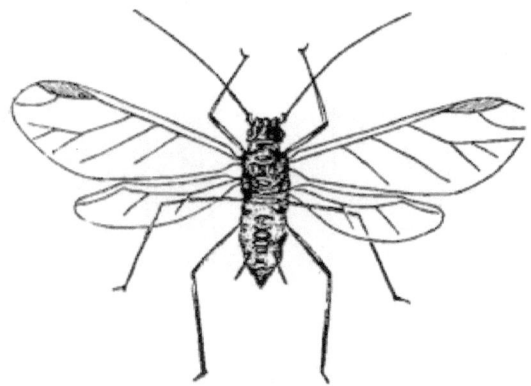

NO. 7
The Hop Aphis, with wings greatly enlarged, (perfect fly).

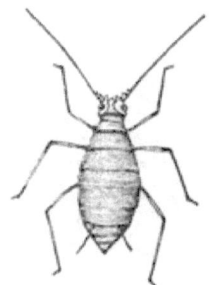

NO. 8
The Hop Aphis (perfect louse), without wings, as shown in cut No. 8.

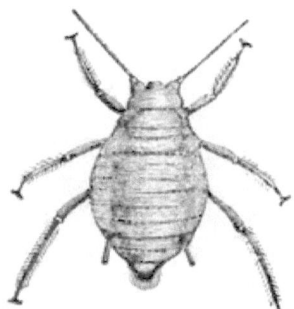

NO. 9
The Plum Louse (or Aphis) as shown in cut No. 9.

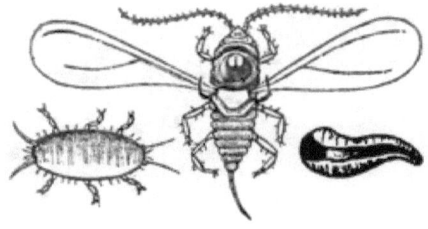

NO. 10
Oyster Shell Scale (perfect fly and larvæ with shell turned bottom side up, where the eggs are to be found concealed.

NO 11
Showing a twig badly infested with the Oyster Shell Scale (or bark louse.)

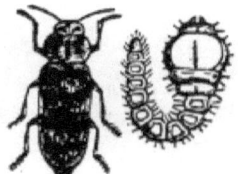

NO. 12
Showing perfect bug and offspring of the Flat-headed Apple Tree Borer, that works between the bark and wood of the apple and other trees.

Engravings by J. T. Clague, Seattle

INDEX.

A

	Page
Author's Life	7
A Recent Visit to Some of the Hop Fields of Washington	45
A New Enemy of Washington Hops	48
A Pest Exterminator in California	68
Apple Maggot	96
Apple Tree Borer	88
Arizona	141

B

Brown's Favorite Prescription	26
Black Spot	39
Bark Bound Trees	44
Brown Apricot Scale	108
British Columbia	142

C

Codlin Moth	83
Canker or Measuring Worm	84
Cabbage Moth	87
Cabbage Aphis	87
Cut Worms	94
Cherry and Pear Tree Slug	95
Clothes Moths	98
Cherry Tree Aphis	102
Chicken Lice and Mites	103
Cattle Lice	104
Chaff Scale	112
Chemist's Certificate	143
California	141
Cuts	165 to 172

D

Destruction of the Fruit Crop	51
Death to Tree Pests	66
Discourse on Injurious Insects	70

E

	Page
Entomology	11
Elm Tree Beetle	90

F

Fertilizers	20
Fungus Diseases	44
Fruit Tree Pests in Utah	57
Fall Web Worm	85
Florida Red Scale	110
Frosted Scale	111

G

Grasshoppers	40
Gooseberry and Currant Worm	96
Green Aphis	98
Grow Your Own Tobacco	121

I

Introductory	5
Insect Pests in Seattle	53
Idaho	139

L

Life and Habits of Ants	74
Leaf Crumplers	91
Leaf Spot Diseases of the Plum and Cherry Trees	105
Lemon Scale	112

N

No Black-hearted Trees in my Grandfather's Orchard	30
No More Pests	61

O

Oyster Shell Scale	106
Other Remedies	122
Oregon	138

P

Planting an Orchard	13
Peach Yellows	37
Peach Tree Borer	89
Potato Bugs	92
Plum Curculio	97
Peach Tree Aphis	101
Plum Tree Aphis	102
Plum Rot	104

	Page
Powderly Mildew of the Cherry	105
Phylixera	107
Purple Scale	112
Prof. Brown's Insecticides	117
Prof. Brown's Favorite Prescription	26

R

Rose Beetle	90
Rose Saw Fly	95
Remedy for Mildew	104
Red Scale	113

S

Spraying	26
Squash Bugs	91
San Jose Scale	105
State Boards of Horticulture	142

T

The Fruit of Boise Basin	43
The Insecticide	23
Treatment of Old Trees	29
Twig Blight	33
Tomato Blight	36
Trees Have the Grip	63
The Hop Pest	71
Tent Caterpillar	85
Thrips	92
The Plum Gouger	93
The Hop Louse	103
The Red Spider	109
Formula	117
The Great Devolopers	137
Testimonials	143

U

Utah	140

W

What is Claimed For It	25
Why Fruit Trees Die	59
Works Like a Charm	68
White Spotted Tussock Moth	86
Wire Worms	91
Woolly Aphis	99
Washington	137

www.ingramcontent.com/pod-product-compliance
Lightning Source LLC
Chambersburg PA
CBHW020259170426
43202CB00008B/439